Seasons of My Life

RICKY CLEMONS

Copyright © 2018 by Ricky Clemons

All rights reserved. No part of this book may be reproduced or transmitted in any form or by any means, electronic or mechanical, including photocopying, recording, or any information storage and retrieval system, without permission in writing from the author.

ISBN: 978-1-948638-96-8

PUBLISHED BY

Fideli Publishing, Inc.
119 W. Morgan St.
Martinsville, IN 46151

www.FideliPublishing.com

Table of Contents

Seasons of My Life i
Table of Contents iii
The Glory and Praise 1
I Am Here 2
Like a Dream 3
All I Have to Do 4
The Truth Can Hurt Sometimes 5
We Can't Point Our Finger 6
God is Not a Man 7
Can Get All Things Done 8
I Know That I Can 9
Before People See 10
Down to Earth 11
There is a Cost to Pay 12
Pride Can Cause Us To 13
Thankful Unto the Lord 14
Our Eyes Can't See the Unseen 15
We are Jesus' Foster Children 16
Showing Them Some Love 17
We Must Ask 18
This Christian Journey 19
God Is 20
Helping Me to Understand 21
It's About What You Want 22
Can Be So Vain 23
When I Think About You 24
I've Never Seen You 25
Can Fly 26
Going Through the Motions of Life 27
In This Lifetime 28
Only Jesus Can Always Judge 29
Can Make You and Me 30
Many People Will Live For 31
Throughout the Years 32
Whiter Than 33
Jesus Knows 34

There is Salvation	35
Our Choices	36
We Should Be Counting Our Blessings	37
Jesus Can Guarantee Us	38
Love	39
We Must Have a Relationship	40
Jesus Will Never Change	41
We Can Ask Jesus	42
Can Go to Church for Years and Years	43
Jesus Can Cleanse	44
O Lord You are With Me	45
Power Me Up	46
We Live in an Unfair World	47
Keep Your Eyes on Jesus	48
Who is Your Master?	49
I Am All Alone	50
Life is Precious	51
Close to Us	52
Can't Get Rid of Spiritual Things	53
Our Foggy Moments in Life	54
Love is a Sure Thing	55
Life Don't Owe Us Anything	56
I Love Being Where I'm at Today	57
I Am Like	58
Will Go By Us	59
Will Fall Short	60
The Ways of Time	61
True Happiness	62
Can Come Upon Us	63
Carry Us Through	64
Can't Add To and Take Out	65
We Must Wait	66
Just Imagine	67
If We Try to Work Our Way	68
In the Big Picture	69
In the Sunset of Time	70
The Activities of Life	71
Love Keeps Me Going	72

Is With Oneself	73
Life is Like	74
Over the Years	75
In Our Lives	76
I Am Rich	77
Life is About	78
This World is Not My Home	79
Energize My Life	80
The Grass is Greener in Jesus	81
Mysterious As	82
You Are Every Good Thing	83
Some Things We Must Overlook	84
Shines Over	85
I Thank You for Using Me	86
If it's Not in God's Word	87
Hold Onto	88
Jesus is Forever and Ever	89
Can Come and Go	90
Paradise in You	91
A Lot of People	92
I Need To	93
It's Not Me	94
My Own Heart	95
It's Always Good	96
It Doesn't Take Much	97
Are You and I Ready?	98
Burdens Will Fly Away	99
There is a Good Kind of Fear	100
Short of Your Glory	101
Is the Free Will Choice a Wrong Thing?	102
Looking Out for Me	103
Strong Love	104
The Lord Will Wait for Us	105
O Lord, You Use	106
Another Moment	107
On the Outside and the Inside	108
Jesus Says	109
We Can Be Doubtful	110

Close to Jesus	111
It's a Miracle	112
If There Was No Law	113
Be Still	114
Only Once in a Lifetime	115
Believing in Jesus	116
It's a Blessing	117
You and I Don't Need	118
Will Always Be Up Against Something	119
Can Seem to be Forever	120
Our Ways Can	121
We Can Create Our Own Tornado	122
Let's Be Real	123
All We Can Do	124
The Lord Can Use Anybody	125
The Church is Not Hollywood	126
God is a Miracle	127
Love is Thicker	128
O Lord Help Me	129
The Heart	130
I Am So Glad	131
We All Have	132
Doing My Own Thing	133
Spreading the Gospel	134
The Most Powerful Thing on Earth	135
The Higher Up	136
Who is All	137
Going Through the Motions of Life	138
You Will Protect Me	139
Jesus Will Not Forget	140
Moving Too Fast	141
It's Easy to Feel Like	142
Jesus Will	143
Having Peace with the Lord	144
We Can't Make Any Excuse	145
It's What We Put In	146
God is in Control	147
The Lord's Ways	148

I Will Be Surprised	149
We Can't Run and Hide	150
If Things are Comfortable All the Time	151
Don't Worship the Church	152
Spiritual Support	153
Freedom	154
Prayer Time	155
Words Are Powerful	156
Is Like Chasing the Wind	157
A Supernatural Thing	158
I Can't Cast a Stone	159
Can Run Deep	160
Can't Save Us from Our Sins	161
Behind	162
The Book of All Truth	163
It Doesn't Take Much Effort	164
We Will Have Some Problems	165
The Master of Our Destiny	166
A Shadow Will Let Us Know	167
We Can Always Be Certain About Jesus	168
Is Only Promised Through	169
Walk Away	170
I Will Trust You, O Lord	171
Some Things are Best Not Said	172
Something is Wrong with Everyone	173
Jesus Can Show Up	174
A Better World to Come	175
That's Just the Way It Is	176
One True Color	177
Go With the Flow of Life	178
Forever and Ever	179
Who am I?	180
We Can Shorten Our Own Lives	181
A Wandering Moment	182
Predestined	183
Whether You're Rich or Poor	184
No Matter	185
We Can See with Our Eyes	186

The Highest Life 187
There is No Distance in Love 188
The Thorn in My Flesh 189
Flip Through the Pages of Life 190
Spiritual Kinfolks 191
Who We Hang Out With 192
Know There is a God 193
Being Full 194
How Did God Begin? 195
A Language that Everyone Can Speak 196
So Quiet 197
God is the Smartest One 198
No One Can Rehearse Life 199
If God 200
We All 201
We Need the Lord's Vaccine 202
The Greatest Social Person 203
Man Cannot Live by Man Alone 204
Discover 205
On the Edge 206
Before We 207
Free as the Wind 208
Will Move 209
The Human Body 210
The Unseen 211
We are Not Ancient 212
There is a Place that We've Never Seen 213
The Eyes of love 214
No Matter 215
Was the Only Thing 216
So Caught Up 217
Can Change Our Life Forever 218
A Spiritual Uplifting 219
A Big Difference 220
The Lord Has Brought Us Through 221
Nature is a Church 222
A Cool Shade 223
Storms in the Heart 224

No Matter How Many Times 225
There is Nothing Right About 226
Can Explore 227
We are All Free 228
If We 229
Life Can't Promise Us 230
The Cross 231
Can Cause 232
Community Service 233
I am Your Mirror 234
To Forgive is to Heal 235
You and I Can Control 236
We Will Be Eternal One Day 237
Music Was Originated 238
The King of 239
Can't Get Rid of God 240
If you Want to Know 241
Great All By Himself 242
A Witness of Jesus 243
In the Blood 244
Make Jesus Look Good 245
The Rocks are Preaching the Truth 246
In the Family of God 247
It's How We Handle Our Blessings 248
Jesus Walked with Me 249
When I was Living in Darkness 250
No One Can Get Higher Than God 251
The Church is Moving 252
Right Now 253
Working It Out 254
The Lord is Always Ahead of Us 255
God is God in Nature 256
In this Sinful World 257
Who Else Can I Talk to Better? 258
I can Only Trust the Lord 259
The Seat Belts of My Life 260
Your Holy Spirit, O Lord 261
We Can Have No Idea 262

Everybody Has a Presence	263
Heaven is Drawing Nearer	264
Over Temporary Things	265
My Spirit is Willing	266
To Uplift Jesus' Name	267
I Must Walk Alone	268
You Are	269
Jesus Will Never Fail	270
There Is No Way Out	271
Cannot Flatter	272
Will I follow the Crowd or Will I Stand Alone?	273
Belongs to the Lord	274
One Thing in Common	275
Jesus Will Always Know	276
There are Mosquito People	277
There is No Weight	278
Life's Best Friend	279
An Island	280
Making Adjustments	281
Run Away	282
To Swirl Up	283
Jesus Plans	284
A Park	285
Are Built	286
We Can Think and Believe That We Are Something	287
Can Raise a Nation	288
Life Can Teach Us	289
The False Church	290
Many People Will	291
How Would We Know?	292
Hungry For …	293
Our Way and Not the Lord's Way	294
Bible Stories	295
Everyone has a Right	296
The Bible Will Tell Us	297
Time is Winding Up Fast	299
Believe in Me and You Shall be Saved	300
I Am	301

Title	Page
Our Conscious	302
Young is Forever	304
We Can Listen	305
An Enemy Within	306
Gone Beyond the Point of No Return	307
The Church is Not About the Creature	308
We Can Lay Down and Rest	309
Great	310
So Extraordinary	311
A Reality Check from the Lord	312
Go and Tell People	314
We Should Never Act Like…	315
Depart From Me, I Never Knew You	316
No Excuse to Sin Against the Lord	317
Satan Called God a Liar	318
In the Universe of Our Hearts	319
Woman	320
From One Place to the Next Place	321
Light	322
Wise Up	323
Countless Raindrops	324
Jesus Gave	325
There is No Abandonment in the Lord	326
If Jesus Had	327
Who, What, When, Where, How and Why	328
The Beauty of Wisdom	329
Should Not be Surprised	330
All the Hardships	331
Will Not Change	332
Will Flow	333
Visitor	334
Jesus is the Truth	335
Will Disappear	336
Time	337
Caught Up	338
Kindness	339
There is Never Enough	340
Can Talk	341

Does the Lord Ever Get Tired?	342
In All of Us	343
No One but You and Your Partner	344
The New Jerusalem Holy City	346
We Can	347
On the Run	348
Nothing To and Something To	349
Addicted	350
There is No Way to Get Around	351
Promise	352
We Christians	353
Broken	354
A Trial Date with God	355
If We Don't Say	356
Jesus	357
Our Works	358
In the Sand of My Life	359
Is Like the Wide-Open Sky	360
Our Purpose	361
Life Can Make Us	362
Jesus Wants Our All	363
We can't Chase Behind Time	364
Who Can Be More?	365

The Glory and Praise

Many people will get out of debt and will give money the glory and praise while they live.

Jesus blessed them to work and get out of debt that is running to and fro throughout the land

Many people will give medicine the glory and praise after they get well, when Jesus spared their life to make a way for them to take the medicine and stay well day after day.

Many people will give man the glory and praise for saving their life, when it was Jesus Christ our Lord who gave them life, health and the strength to save lives.

So many people are going to the grave being lost in their sins for not giving Jesus Christ the glory and praise during their lives.

Many people are living well with money and health and won't give Jesus any glory and praise.

Jesus gives breath to all to live above the deep pits of death

All the glory and praise belongs to Jesus, who will never do us wrong.

I Am Here

I am here in my moment in time that the Lord gives to me to search and find Him with all my heart.

I am here in the land of the living in the new year that the Lord has given to me according to his will.

I am here, existing above the grave because Jesus gave me a chance to be saved in him, who knows better than anyone else why I am here.

I am here to love and obey Jesus, whose all seeing eyes will watch over my soul on my good days and bad days.

I am here because of Jesus Christ, who I can always pray to and get a peace of mind

To know why I am here, existing from birth to this day that will go away

Why I am here to be destined to be saved or lost, that is my free will choice that Jesus gave to me.

I am still here to choose to worship Jesus and keep his ten golden rules, making my destiny sure for heaven.

I am here to do God's will and not my own will that has no power to make me be here.

Life comes from Jesus, who paid my price to save me from my sins.

Like a Dream

The hard times that we've been through are like a dream that passes through the night and fades away so as it seems in the early morning sunlight.

Jesus Christ can lead our dreams into his resting place where life is more abundant.

What we go through is like a dream that Jesus can pass away in the night.

Hours of our trials can cause you and me to spiritually sleepwalk away from Jesus, who will forever be our Lord and Savior.

The Lord rules over dreams to set us free from nightmares that can kill us dead if we don't trust Jesus and obey Him.

He will lead us and guide us through all the things that we go through.

Life will only be like a dream that will come and go away from you and me, thanks to Jesus who won't let the dreams hang around us and get us down, especially not on His holy ground.

All I Have to Do

All I have to do is sit back and see your power, O Lord, working its way through every second, minute, and hour of the day and night.

All I have to do is to sit back and see your power, O Lord, moving through people's lives being attacked by things that will fail them

Your power, O Lord, is sure protection for all who will do Your holy will day after day.

All I have to do is to sit back and see Your power, Lord Jesus, setting the captives free.

To love and obey you with a whole heart, all I have to do is sit back and see your power, O Lord, that will chew up and spit out selfishness.

Your righteousness does no one wrong under the sky and beyond the sky.

All I have to do is see your power, O Lord, doing what I can't do and preparing me to be saved before I die.

Your power will raise me from the dead to get my reward.

All I have to do is see your power, O Lord, bringing the church to one accord.

The Truth Can Hurt Sometimes

The truth can hurt sometimes, but a lie can always hurt us and can blind our eyes to not see the truth that is Jesus.

Jesus will never hurt our hearts with His holy word that you and I can always trust to set us free from lies that can always hurt us.

The truth can hurt if we are living our lives in sin that Jesus paid for on the cross with the price that we cannot pay for our sins.

Our sins are telling lies to us each and every day.

Even a fool wouldn't doubt the truth will set him free.

Jesus never told lies to anyone when he lived on earth and died to save souls from being lost in the devil's lies.

The truth can hurt us and set us free from lies that can come into the church.

We Can't Point Our Finger

We can't point our finger at people's open sins that we see day after say.

We may have some secret sins, so we should not point our finger at other people's open sins.

Sin is sin to Jesus, who once lived without sin in this world.

Only He is worthy to point His finger at our sins, no matter who we are or where we live.

That doesn't matter to Jesus, who sees every open and secret sin each and everyday upon the land of the living.

We are not worthy to point our finger at people sins.

A sinner can repent and get full of the power of the Holy Spirit and love Jesus and keep his commandments of love.

You and I have sins, whether they're open or secret.

The devil, who has no power over our free will, wants us to point at one another.

Only Jesus can cleanse our sins non-stop.

God is Not a Man

God is not a man.

God's Son became a sinless man, to redeem man back to God so that man can be saved and go to heaven to be with God forever and ever.

Adam did depart from God, who is not a man.

Many people will look at a man like he's a god living in this world.

Sin could not enter into the sinless man, Jesus Christ, who came to this world to represent God for man to know that God loves man.

Man is not God.

God is so holy, perfect, righteous, forgiving and omnipotent above man.

Man is not God.

God is love and all-powerful and without sin.

Man is not love when God is love giving love to man.

No man, woman, boy or girl is God.

Man is meant to worship God.

Can Get All Things Done

Money can get a lot of things done.

The Lord can get *all* things done that money can't do upon the land.

Education can get a lot of things done.

The Lord can get *all* things done that education can't do in this world.

Skills can get a lot of things done.

The Lord can get *all* things done that skills can't do from sun up to sun down.

Helping hands can get a lot of things done.

The Lord can get *all* things done and not leave anything out of his blessings.

The Lord helps the helping hands to help others move on in life and greatly step out to do much better in life.

Love can get a lot of things done.

The Lord is love from heaven above and gets *all* things done for us.

We can never get enough of what Jesus can do for us, he will never run out of good things to get all good things done.

I Know That I Can

I know that I can easily fall into the devil's temptation on any day.

I know that I am not better than anyone who can easily fall into the devil's temptations.

Jesus Christ, our Lord, overcame all of the devil's temptations with power and glory given to him.

He helps me not to fall into the devil's temptations that are around twenty-four hours around the clock.

I need Jesus to give me the strength to not think impure thoughts that will surely do my mind so wrong each and every day.

The devil will try to cause me to sin against Jesus, who says, "If you love Me, you will keep My commandments."

The devil also knows but cannot keep me from Jesus, who gave me a cross to carry in the price he paid for all my sins.

Before People See

Before people see Jesus in the Bible they must see Jesus in you and me, who will have selfless ways if we love and obey Jesus.

We should be a living sermon that people need to see before picking up a Bible to study about Jesus Christ.

People would rather see Jesus living in you and me without a doubt, so they can know He is real in the world.

Never feed a spiritual babe, spiritual meat. That won't be good to digest.

Spiritual milk is good for spiritual babes, who need to see Jesus in you and me on our good days and bad days.

We must represent Jesus before people see Him in the Bible so they will be encouraged to read the Bible and see what a friend we have in Jesus, who can save us from our sins.

Down to Earth

Some people are so high up in talking about spiritual things that they don't know how to use the common sense the Lord gave them to meet people where they are, which might be on a spiritual low.

You and I need to come down to earth for people to know that Jesus Christ, our Lord, was also down to earth and met people where they were in their issues with life on the streets and in their homes.

Jesus was very spiritual and very down to earth.

He reached out his hand and healed the sick, fed the hungry and cast out demons day after day.

Some people are so high up in spiritual things that they don't use their God-given common sense to be seen by people who may want to be understood by what they say and do.

We should always be down to earth for Jesus to meet us and take us on a spiritual high to wait on Him to work things out for us in his perfect time.

Jesus leads sinners to his church.

There is a Cost to Pay

There is a cost to pay to be a Christian.

Christians will go through some bad times for following Jesus through the thick and thin of life.

There is a cost to pay for not being of the world and being different day after day.

We Christians love to obey God's ten golden rule.

We do it because we love Jesus, who paid the highest cost for you and me.

Day after day there is a cost to pay for doing God's will by living right in this world where sin is real.

Sin tries to separate us from Jesus Christ, who's our Lord and Savior. He gave up His life and rose from the grave for all the world to be saved

Everyone will not pay their cost, deny self and pick up their cross to follow Jesus around the clock.

There is a cost to pay. We must suffer in the flesh for Jesus' name's sake.

That is the best thing a Christian can do. Make no mistake.

Jesus will give us the victory to overcome the weakness in our flesh.

Many people don't believe this to be true.

From day to day, there is a cost to pay to be a Christian.

Jesus will give us strength to hold onto Him, and He will judge this world fairly.

Pride Can Cause Us To

Pride can cause us to sink and drown in the sea of self for taking our eyes off of Jesus, who didn't let Peter drown.

Like Peter who let himself down for taking his eyes off of Jesus for being proud as he looked back at the disciples while he walked on the water that roared.

The Lord knew that Peter would get full of pride for walking on the water in the storm.

You and I must keep our eyes on Jesus Christ, who used the storm to stop his disciples from complaining about His refusing to set up his kingdom to rule over a nation of leaders who were full of pride.

Pride can cause us to take our eyes off of Jesus and begin to believe we're self-made.

Jesus has made us who we are and we should humble ourselves before Him day after day.

Pride can cause us to spiritually decay for leaning to our own ways.

Thankful Unto the Lord

If we are always thankful unto the Lord, we won't worry when our money get short.

We will know not to spend on things that we may not need.

If we are always thankful unto the Lord, we won't worry about what we don't have.

The Lord will see fit to bless us with more things in his time if we trust and obey Him day after day under the sunshine.

If we are always thankful unto our Lord and Savior Jesus Christ, we won't worry about what we have no control over in this life.

Our past, present and future is in Jesus' almighty hand.

We should always be thankful that Jesus can give us the strength to overcome our trails so we can make a stand for Him.

We can always be thankful to Him upon this sinful land where so many people are not thankful unto the Lord because they believe they made themselves prosper by leaning to their own ways.

The Bible says to always give thanks unto Jesus, both on our good days and on our bad days.

Jesus can get us through everything, because He walked in our shoes.

Our Eyes Can't See the Unseen

Our eyes can't see the unseen because of being born in sin.

Sin covers our eyes and keeps us from seeing the unseen.

We've never seen God, whose son Jesus Christ was once seen here on earth.

Jesus lived a sinless life

Our eyes can't see the unseen here on earth and in heaven on high.

We can only see the things that are temporary. Unseen things are eternal.

Unseen things are kept from you and me by the sin that covers our eyes.

Our eyes can't see the unseen all around us, but we can always love and worship the unseen God on His holy ground.

What is seen is the fruit of His spirit in you and me right now.

We are the seen church of an unseen Lord and Savior, who gives us His seen favor.

We are Jesus' Foster Children

We are Jesus' foster children who He will accept and raise up in His saving grace.

He loves us no matter what age we are as long as we grow to love Him and obey his golden rules.

We foster children can choose what we do in this world that's not our real home.

Jesus has adopted us to one day go with Him above the sky dome.

Heaven is our real home to be with our Heavenly Father, God, who loves to shower us with His love. Earthly parents can abandon us and leave us all alone in our grief, making us not trust anyone.

We can always trust Jesus Christ to love us and supply all of our needs in this life, and in the eternal life to one day come to all.

We foster children are called by God to be saved in His Son, Jesus Christ, who is our spiritual foster parent.

He has no sins for us to question Him about all through our lives.

We are all foster children in this world that's not our real home that God will destroy in the end because of sin.

Showing Them Some Love

Many people don't care about how rich you are.

Many people care about you showing them some love from your heart.

Jesus will give us His love each and every day.

Many people don't care about how good you look.

You are not worth a penny to them if you don't show them some love.

Jesus gives love to you day after day from heaven above.

Many people don't care about how talented you are.

They care about you showing them some love to catch their full attention.

No matter where you live, Jesus wants to live in your heart for you to love him the most and know what love really is all through your life.

Many people don't care about how smart that you are.

They care about you showing them some love to cover a multitude of sins.

Jesus covered our sins on the cross. He loves all souls that He created, great and small, who can choose to show some love.

We Must Ask

We must ask the Lord for things, and if it's His will He will give us what we ask of Him.

We should not be too proud to ask the Lord for things.

A lot of things are not good for us and the Lord won't give them to us.

We should not be too proud to ask one another for things that we need.

According to the Lord's will we should give one another what we need.

The Lord says that we don't have something because we don't ask Him for wisdom, healing and spiritual things

He always knows why we are so doubtful to trust Him who can give us what we ask for.

It's in His will.

We will truly see that Jesus is not hard on us by not giving us what we ask for.

When we are sleeping in our beds, Jesus is answering our prayers to open a door that may have been closed on us.

This Christian Journey

This Christian journey is not easy no matter what anyone says.

There is a straight and narrow road, like the Bible says about this Christian journey.

We can stumble or may fall in some kind of way that Jesus always sees.

This Christian journey is not always easy to walk on when the devil is trying to tempt us to stop praying and believing in Jesus Christ.

Our Christian journey is all about Jesus giving us the power to hold onto him and keep on trying to live right by His holy law.

He won't burden us down under the sky.

This Christian journey will lighten our heavy load of falling short of the glory of God, who is the ancient of days of old and the present and future.

God is one with Jesus Christ, who has won the victory for us to stay on this Christian journey for life.

God Is

God is a spiritual God who will give us His holy spirit if we choose to live our lives doing his holy will. His son, Jesus, did this when He lived here on earth without committing any sin against God.

God is a reality God who wants you and me to live in the real world with the bad things that we see day in and day out.

God is a loving God and a forgiving God who gives us chances and chances to repent and stand on his holy word to live our lives loving him.

His son, Jesus Christ, can save our souls from being lost in sin that will always do us in with deception, lies, sickness, sorrow and death.

God is the breath of life upon our health for our soul to prosper, especially in spiritual wealth.

Helping Me to Understand

I thank you, O Lord, for helping me to understand what is going on with me, even though I can disobey You and make excuses about it.

You pity on me and give me Your holy spirit of truth to set me free to see what a wretch I am.

I need you, O Lord, to help me to understand myself, who will fall short of your glory in some kind of way each and everyday.

You will always do what you say, even though I may not understand what is going on.

I will do what you say, which is always right by You, my Lord and Savior Jesus Christ.

I truly thank You for helping me to understand what is going on with me.

I am like a blank sheet of paper without you, my Lord, writing your holy law in my heart that needs your understanding through thick and thin.

Throughout my life I know that You, O Lord, will always understand me and cleanse me of my sins.

It's About What You Want

It's not about what I want.

It's about what you want me to do, O Lord, who will bless me without a doubt for doing what You want me to do.

It's not about what I don't want to do.

It's about what you want, O Lord.

I try to do what is always good for me, even when I don't see the blessings in what You, O Lord, want me to do.

You open my eyes for me to see Your will to be done and not my will that can blind my spiritual eyes to the hidden treasures.

What You, O Lord, want me to do will glorify You, my Lord Jesus, who has my reward in Your almighty hands.

You are always ready to give me more of Your blessings if I do what You want me to do all through my life.

You, my Lord, want me to keep Your law.

Can Be So Vain

Our talk can be so vain if the name of Jesus Christ is not spoken on our tongues to speak of an abundance of life being about Jesus.

Our actions can be so vain if we are not doing good things in Jesus' name that is above and beyond our names.

Doing this can bring on doubt and dislike upon the land of the living that Jesus owns each and every day.

Our hearts can be so vain if our motives are far away from being about Jesus.

Our hearts have no good motives without Jesus cleansing us of our sins that we must repent.

Our lives can be so vain if we don't love Jesus and keep his golden rules that are so vain to wicked people wherever we go.

When I Think About You

When I think about you, O Lord, I feel on top of this world that is all about giving me a bad deal in life. You, my Lord Jesus Christ, command me to live my life doing Your holy will, day after day.

Your blessings are upon me because when I think about You, O Lord, my mind is clear of selfish thoughts that won't do me any good.

When I think about You, O Lord, there is no room for sin to enter into my mind to tempt me to sin against you.

My Lord, You can set me free from foolish thoughts.

When I think about You, my Lord, You take my mind high above this world to your sinless place beyond the sky.

I've Never Seen You

I've never seen you fail me, O Lord.

You cannot do that.

I've never seen You do me wrong, O Lord, who will always do me right my whole life long.

In this world I've never seen You leave me or forsake me, O Lord, who I can always lean on.

You get me through the day and the night.

I've never seen You deceive me, O Lord, who will fight my battles for me and will always win.

I've never seen You, my Lord Jesus, not forgive me of my sins.

I confess and repent unto You, my best friend.

O Lord, I've never seen You not giving me a chance over and over again to choose to do Your will and advance to spiritual heights in You.

Can Fly

Birds can fly.

Our thoughts can fly with motives not about the Lord in heaven on high above the birds that can fly high up in the sky.

Our tongues can fly with words not about the Lord, whose words are always holy and right without a doubt.

Birds can fly high above our actions that can fly in doing something wrong that the Lord always sees as sin.

These actions cause us to look so guilty before the Lord Jesus Christ, who created the birds to fly.

Jesus created the birds to fly above the seashores and hilltops and mountains.

Our hearts can fly with selfish ways, but if we are with the Lord, the Lord will fly His salvation around the world for all to be saved.

Going Through the Motions of Life

We will only go through the motions of life if we don't love and obey Jesus Christ, who gives our lives true meaning.

Only going through the motions of life will sooner or later weigh us down with not being fulfilled.

The things we have can't give us joy and peace like Jesus can.

He wants us to live in this world and be happy about doing His holy will.

That is so much better than only going through the motions of life, which can surely chew us up with stress and depression.

We should not be holding on to temporary things that can't save our souls.

Only Jesus can make our lives complete.

When we're only going through the motions of life we can get the blues.

Jesus can make our lives renewed in Him who is forever greater than going through the motions of life.

In This Lifetime

In this lifetime, we must be saved in Jesus to live in the afterlife.

The graves will be opened for the righteous to be raised from their sleep to go to heaven with Jesus Christ.

The righteous living will change from mortal to immortality in the twinkling of an eye.

All sin will be erased from our lives for being saved in Jesus.

In this lifetime we must live for Jesus, day after day, as if this is the only life we have to live.

Jesus will give us eternal life for doing His holy will.

In this lifetime we need to get filled with the Holy Spirit to seal us for the afterlife with our Lord and Savior Jesus Christ.

We must confess and repent of our sins unto Him in this lifetime that will come to an end.

Only Jesus Can Always Judge

Only Jesus Christ can always judge you and me, right and fair because he knows our whole hearts

He will always see and judge our motives and intents, even though you and I don't always see this in one another.

We should not judge one another's hearts or bring out good words for the wrong reasons.

Without a doubt, Jesus always sees so crystal clear.

Only Jesus was without sin, so He can judge even judge the sneers on our faces before we say and do anything right or wrong.

We are not always right about what we see with our eyesight.

We can come up with our own opinion that maybe so wrong.

Only Jesus can always judge you and me who have sins to confess and repent of unto Him.

He is the judge of the beginning and the end of our lives.

Jesus will judge us for doing good or evil, no matter what neighborhood we live in.

Can Make You and Me

Nobody can make you and me feel so good like Jesus does.

He always knows that we should trust him to make a good thing out of any bad thing that comes our way.

Jesus can bring us so much joy and peace because we know that Jesus will not fail us, no matter where we are in our lives.

Nobody can make you and me feel so good like Jesus can make us feel.

When we are ill or well, we can always pray to Jesus.

He is always on time, even when we see no way through the day.

Jesus can bring His sunshine of blessings to make you and me feel so good and brand new.

Many People Will Live For

Many people will live for who they see and not live by faith in Jesus who they don't see.

It is vain for them to do this.

Jesus is real and there to have a relationship with each and every day.

Many people will live for the things they see and say that they're real and will satisfy their souls.

Jesus gives us life, health and strength so that we can trust we will live on beyond the material things that have no life to give us.

Only our Lord Jesus Christ can give this to us.

Many people will live for how much they can get in life and will never want to reach out and touch the contentment that Jesus gives to all who put their trust in Him.

Many people will live for their unrepented sins.

Jesus can forgive us our sins and save us from them if we live for Him who came to this world without sin.

Throughout the Years

Throughout the years, the Lord has brought me this far and that is too much for me to see and wonder about.

Throughout the years of my life there were times that I didn't fear the Lord.

I didn't think that I would ever do His holy will, even when the Lord was near to me.

He brought me this far beyond my selfish ways that I was stuck in for a long time.

Throughout the years, I was so wrong to not love Jesus who loved me when I didn't love him.

He heard my cries of longing for what I didn't have that he could always give to me.

Throughout the years, my sins would have destroyed my soul if Jesus wasn't so good to me.

Throughout the years, Jesus stood up for me to be saved.

Whiter Than

Our pure white robes will be whiter than the snow that can look so beautiful upon the land.

Our pure white robes will be whiter than the clouds in the sky that we can't touch with our hands.

We can put our hands together and pray to Jesus Christ, who will give us our pure white robes through the price that he paid for us to be saved from our sins.

Our pure white robes will be whiter than the full white moon shining every hour over the fields.

Jesus will give us a pure white robe for loving and obeying Him who is always right with God.

He makes us his holy children in God's eyes.

Jesus Knows

We don't know all the ways of love that Jesus knows from heaven above.

We don't know all the ways of wisdom that Jesus knows beyond the sunlight rays.

Below the sky there is foolishness in the nature of men who were born to sin against God.

We don't know and in every way we fall short of His glory.

We are all called by Jesus Christ to repent and turn away from our sins.

We don't know all the ways of sin under the sun, but Jesus knows because He bore all of our sins and became sin on the cross to take our place.

We don't know all the games the devil can play on us, but Jesus knows and will help us to be so cautious and victorious in this world wherever we go.

There is Salvation

There is salvation in Jesus Christ.

There is no salvation in Hollywood that can't bear our sins.

Jesus did bear them.

There is no salvation in the government being so corrupt today with leaders living in so much sin.

Only Jesus can save us from sin when the end of this world is coming soon.

There is no salvation in the church where many people's hearts are not right with God from the start of the day to the end of the day and into the night.

There is salvation in Jesus Christ, but not in the military with soldiers getting wounded and killed with their blood dripping upon the land.

Our Choices

Our choices are a matter of life or death.

Good choices prolong life in the breath that we breathe to live especially to do the Lord's will.

The Lord gave you and me a free will to also make bad choices that can shorten our life by the mistakes we make.

Our choices are a matter of life or death that stick like glue to our hearts.

Jesus defines what choices we make, 24 hours around the clock.

Our choices are a matter of life or death when we can choose to live our life under Jesus Christ.

We Should Be Counting Our Blessings

We should be counting our blessings and not be worrying about who's talking bad about us.

The Lord sees who to bless so we shouldn't worry about who doesn't like us.

We can count our blessings from the Lord, who we can trust to always work out our problems.

No problem is bigger than the Lord.

We shouldn't worry about who may stop loving us.

Jesus Christ, our Lord, loves with an unfailing love from heaven on high above.

A sinner's love can fail us.

We should be counting our blessings and not worry about who's not good to us.

Jesus, our Lord, is good to us all the time.

We should be counting our blessings, even though we can't count them all under the sun that greatly shines all around us, great and small.

Jesus Can Guarantee Us

Life can't guarantee us there will be no sickness.

That can come upon us at any time of the day and night.

Life can't guarantee us there will be no disappointments or grief.

Jesus Christ can guarantee to give us hope in Him.

Life can't guarantee us there will be no trials or temptations.

We will go through those no matter where we live.

We can put our trust in Jesus who can guarantee us victory in overcoming the things that can make us weak.

This life can't guarantee we'll be healed.

But if we're saved, we'll receive eternal life in Him who will come back again one day.

This life has no guarantees above the grave.

But the righteous dead are guaranteed to be raised from the dead to be with Jesus in the clouds of glory when His trumpet blows.

Love

Love doesn't always come at first sight.

Love will sometimes come years later at the height of just being good friends.

Love can grow into trust and last through the strong winds that blow.

The Lord always knows that His love will never fail us.

We can never get enough of His love that will always come at first sight of His holy word.

We can see to study about what a friend Jesus will always be to you and me.

We don't know what love is until we love Jesus.

Know that Jesus is always the right one to supply all of our needs in the right way.

Jesus calls us to confess and repent of our sins, and for us to love him.

We can always trust His love at first sight until the end when we go to the dust.

We Must Have a Relationship

We must have a relationship with Jesus Christ to believe that He will answer our prayers.

Doubt can deceive us so we don't believe.

We must have a relationship with Jesus to overcome fear and depression that can slip down in our souls and drug us, making us have no hope.

Jesus has overcome the world for us to cope with our disappointments, heartaches and sorrow.

We must have a relationship with Jesus today so that tomorrow we can look forward to eternity.

We need to have a relationship with Jesus who is so good to us all the time.

We must have a relationship with Jesus to believe that He created us to love Him and keep His golden rules.

Having a relationship with Jesus will cause us to trust Him to get us through, no matter what we go through.

We need to have a relationship with Jesus, even unto death. Jesus will raise the righteous from the grave because Jesus is the breath of life and eternal life.

Jesus Will Never Change

Jesus will never change, but we can change our minds at any time we want to under the sun that shines.

Our bodies will go through some changes as we age and get older. We'll move a little slower than before.

Jesus will never change. He will be the same yesterday, today and tomorrow.

Jesus won't change His mind.

What's written in his holy word will never change.

We change our minds so real, and our ways of doing things can change, too.

We can also change what we say in a minute.

Jesus will never change on you and me, even though we can change on one another as we go through life.

Jesus will one day change this world from old to new, as well as everyone who is saved.

We Can Ask Jesus

We can ask for what we need because Jesus knows what we need better than we will ever know.

We may not know what we need at the right time, but Jesus knows what we need.

Jesus is behind and in front of us to see what we don't see so we don't stumble and fall.

We are so free to choose what we want to say and do that our wants can be a curse to us and surely make us sin against the Lord.

The Lord always knows the difference between our wants and needs.

We can believe that some things are a need but they're really a want in the Lord Jesus Christ's eyes.

We can always ask for what we need in this life, but our wants can cause much pain and strife because we believe that our needs are not enough to satisfy us who can want more things around the clock.

Can Go to Church for Years and Years

Some people can go to church for years and years and have no faith in Jesus, especially if they get sick and near to death.

Jesus can hold back death when some people can go to church for years and years and deliberately disobey the Lord as if there is no holy law to keep day after day.

Some people can go to church for years and years and say nothing much about what Jesus has done for them over the years when they had it hard and their life looked dim.

Some people can go to church for years and years and do nothing in Jesus' name that can make demons tremble in fear.

Some people can go to church for years and years and not want to work out their own soul's salvation. They put their trust in the preacher to do it for them, when the preacher has sins and falls short of the glory of God who gave us His son Jesus to save us from our sins before we go to the dust.

Jesus Can Cleanse

The devil will try to put all kinds of evil thoughts in our minds.

Jesus can cleanse our minds if we think of him all the time.

The devil will never give up on tempting you and me to sin against the Lord who can set us free from living in sin if we confess and repent of our sins.

Jesus shed his precious blood to cleanse us in every way that is possible.

Jesus can do anything but fail you and me.

Jesus can cleanse us all through our lives that we can commit a sin against God who gave us his only begotten Son to bring us back to him.

The devil is always on attack to cause us to fall into sin.

Jesus Christ, Our Lord, can cleanse us of sin and renew our lives.

As we get to know His will for us in his holy word, we can obey to show Jesus that we love Him so the devil will see that we are washed clean in the blood of Jesus who loves you and me.

O Lord You are With Me

O Lord, You are with me in my home,

You won't leave me all alone.

O Lord, You are with me in my trials that help me to see that I need you to help me to get through it.

O Lord, You are with me in the church where I need Your holy spirit to help me to take heed of being in your holy place to worship.

You are representing my case and, O Lord, You are with me to save my soul in your amazing grace.

O Lord, You are with me on my good and bad days and you are with me when I dream away.

Power Me Up

Power me up with your love, O Lord, and encourage me to love you and my neighbors that others will see from day to day

I need to be powered up with your strength, my Lord Jesus Christ. You keep my strong in my faith and works throughout my life.

You, O Lord, can power me up with your joy and peace that makes me smile in a land of troubled times in these last days.

I need to be powered up in your ways, O Lord, when my ways can make me weak and not always do right when things can look so bleak.

You, my Lord, power me up with Your mercy and grace every second, minute and hour of the day.

I need to be powered up with you, Lord Jesus.

We Live in an Unfair World

We live in an unfair world where everyone is not treated right under the sun, in this unfair world where everyone doesn't get what they deserve, we can pray to the Lord and get a fair answer all the time.

Jesus is always fair to shine His light of truth on everyone who needs to hear the truth of His holy word. That is always fair and dear to our souls and can set us free in this unfair world where we don't always get what we deserve.

Jesus is fair to save everyone's soul from being lost in sin that is unfair to everyone wherever we go in this unfair world.

Showing respect to persons can be so unfair, but to all who love Jesus, they will know He is never unfair to find his one lost sheep in this unfair world that's not worth a dime to all who love their neighbors.

That is fair to do under the sunshine where this world wasn't fair to Jesus Christ who is fair all the time.

Keep Your Eyes on Jesus

Keep your eyes on Jesus and not on people who can deceive you in one way or another, day after day.

You must keep your eyes on Jesus and not on people who can let you down a lot.

If you keep your eyes on Jesus you will have a peace of mind, even in this world that is filled with sin breaking God's holy law all the time.

You must keep your eyes on Jesus, who can find you and me and bring us back to Him if we are lost in our sins and hate.

We need to keep our eyes on Jesus, who can open our eyes to see the truth that will set you and me free from deceptive people who can do good works in Jesus' name and then talk bad about you and me.

Who is Your Master?

Who is your master that you will serve day after day?

Nothing in this world is more superb than God, who is a master who will never enslave anyone to do what they don't want to do day after day.

Who is your master that will sooner or later show and tell on yourself so very real?

You and I can reveal by what we say and do and can be in denial.

A dog knows his master to obey under the sign of the rainbow.

This world has many masters.

Who is your master that can tempt you to sin against God who sent his only begotten Son to this world? We need to make Jesus Christ our master who is good all the time to you and me.

We will have no regrets for making Jesus our master. He truly knows to never enslave us to sin.

I Am All Alone

I am all alone to choose to say good words or bad words day after day.

I am all alone to choose to do right or wrong in God's all seeing eyesight that will never overlook all that I say and do.

I am all alone to go through my trials that will make me or break me.

Who is all alone to see that the Lord will always be with me when others may have some doubt?

I am all alone to deny myself and pick up my cross to follow Jesus. No one else can do it for me each and every day.

I am all alone to choose to do good or evil that will make me known to my neighbors who can't choose for me.

I must work out my soul salvation all alone until I return to the dust.

Life is Precious

Life is precious to anyone who loves to save lives — even the lives of animals that God gave to mankind to love and take care of.

Life is precious to our Lord and Savior Jesus Christ, who loves to save souls from being lost.

We all can make a free will choice to view life as precious.

God won't force us to love and obey him, who gave the world His only begotten son.

He gave up his precious life under the bliss of heaven, where life is short and precious to all.

Who loves to live life unto Jesus Christ who calls everyone to confess and repent of our sins?

Life is precious to all who live with their neighbors until the end.

Close to Us

Time will get close to us to let us know that our time could be up at any day.

We can go to the grave without being close to Jesus Christ, who wants to be close to us in our lives.

Temptations will get close to us to tempt us to sin against the Lord, who will not exempt anyone from His saving grace.

Jesus gives this to all to be saved in Him. He lives forever and ever.

The unknown will get close to us who don't know everything that Jesus knows.

We can trust Jesus to bring us close to Him, even in ways that we don't see.

The truth wants to get close to us to set us free from lies that love to get close to you and me.

Can't Get Rid of Spiritual Things

Evolution can't get rid of spiritual things that are written in the Bible to bring us truth about our existence.

Technology can't get rid of spiritual things that come from Jesus Christ who did spiritual things on earth to save many souls from being lost.

Science can't get rid of spiritual things that sin tells lies on day after day.

Spiritual things are also seen in nature that's way below the heavens above where God is a spirit who talks to our hearts through his Holy Spirit who is spiritual like Jesus Christ.

Death can't get rid of spiritual things that life gives to us through the price that Jesus paid for this world to still exist after being weighed down with lies.

The root of sin can't get rid of spiritual things that the devil can't throw down in his pit.

Our Foggy Moments in Life

Our foggy moments in life let us know that we can't always see things so clear.

We need Jesus to show us what it means in our foggy moments in life that can seem so thick with problems hanging over our heads.

We are so blessed to be alive and not dead in the grave where no one can see the fog filling up the sky and moving through the trees.

In our foggy moments, Jesus can set us free

He can clear up our lives with his sunshine of love, truth and grace that we can't get enough of.

Our foggy moments in life are the way Jesus Christ tests our faith in Him who had some foggy moments in his life with rebellious people who didn't see that He also paid their price on the cross with his life.

Love is a Sure Thing

Love is a sure thing to treat us right in everyone's eyesight.

Jesus is love every day and every night. Love will not put up a fuss and fight with anyone who Jesus loves all the time.

That love won't cause any ill feelings.

Love is above anything that might get us down.

Jesus can remove this and lift us up with a love that cannot fail.

Whose love is true like Jesus' love is always true to you and me?

Love will always fall through the cracks in our hearts. Only the love of Jesus can do.

Love is always a sure thing to not fall short of being there for us when we know Jesus Christ, who is the love of God.

Love will never hurt or kill anyone near or far.

Life Don't Owe Us Anything

Life doesn't owe us anything.

We are so blessed to be alive and to live our lives as we choose to live so free.

This is all thanks to the Lord Jesus Christ, who gives us life free of charge.

We can't put a price on life that doesn't owe us anything.

We can see so many young people are dying young, never reach old age.

Life doesn't owe us.

We can shorten our own lives by making bad choices.

That is so known in this life.

No one has any right to take anyone else's life.

We owe a lot to life because of Jesus Christ.

We live for free all through our lives, but life doesn't owe us anything no matter who we are, great and small.

We owe our lives to Jesus near and far, no matter where we live under the sun, moon and stars.

I Love Being Where I'm at Today

I love being where I'm at today.

I am a new creature in Jesus, who I can pray to each and every day.

I don't want to be like I used to be in the past years.

I see the new creature in me who loves being where I am at in my Lord Jesus Christ who truly cared about me being saved in Him as if I was the only sinner.

His eyes didn't look by me, they looked at me.

When I was in my sinful condition during all of those years of living in sin, I hated to see myself.

Where I am at today is because Jesus cast a spiritual net and won my soul.

He has brought me where I'm at today so I can go through my trials on His straight and narrow road.

I Am Like

I am like the open wide sky for people to see what effect that I have on them.

Jesus will help me to have a good effect on those who need it the most.

From day to day I am like the deep ocean of emotions.

This deep may be unknown to many folks, but they will see that I made an oath to Jesus.

I will live in His holy word that sets me free.

I will confess and repent of every seen sin.

I am like the ground that caves in from any earthquake, but Jesus will hold me up to walk on His holy ground.

My soul will be saved in His holy name that flows all through my heart wherever I go.

Will Go By Us

The day will go by us who can't go by Jesus no matter what we do under the sky.

The week will go by us who can't go by Jesus no matter what we know.

The month will go by us who can't go by Jesus no matter what we go through.

As the year will go by us who can't go by Jesus Christ.

Like the day, week, month and year our lives are under the command of Jesus.

Every day, week, month and year we can stay close to Jesus who will not go by us.

We will be saved in Him who we can always trust to never leave us or forsake us even in the dust that we will go back to when life will go by us.

Will Fall Short

Leaves will fall from the trees.

You and I will fall short of the glory of God.

We will see in our words that we are not always being right.

God will never fall short of what He says, every day and night.

His holy word is always right and will never fall short.

The holy angels will forever exhort the Lord Jesus Christ, who did not fall into sin.

A star will fall from the sky over us all, who will fall short of the glory of God.

God loves us all, even though we will fall short in our actions all through our lives.

Jesus cannot fall short to answer our prayers and help us to do right, if we choose to pick up our cross and follow Jesus, who cannot fall short to save us today and tomorrow.

If we do this, we will not fall short or be left dealing with sorrow.

The Ways of Time

The ways of time are from the Lord, who gives us time to come onboard with His salvation.

Jesus gives salvation to all, great and small who are called by the Lord to give their time to Him.

Time can make us to be like precious gems to the Lord, who is always on time.

He works things out for us who live under the sunshine.

The ways of time will never change on the Lord. Our ways can change on the Lord and can change on one another.

We should never take time for granted; time can flee away from us.

We need to go to Jesus Christ, who can put a pause on time to extend us more time to live.

We can think that we have all the time in the world to get it right with Jesus, who lives above time.

It's time to do God's will, but time can't choose this for us to do.

True Happiness

Doing our own thing will not give us true happiness in this world.

We cannot trust anything to give us true happiness except Jesus Christ.

He can give us true happiness if we live our lives doing His will.

We can achieve this only by keeping his ten golden rules.

These are for all men to keep, day after day.

Leaning to our own selfish ways won't give us true happiness.

Anyone saved in Jesus knows that only He will bring us through our hardships.

Nothing will get the best of us in the rip currents of life when Jesus is with us.

Nothing can't stop Jesus from giving us true happiness.

True happiness is Jesus, who knocks on the door of our hearts where no one can make us happy like Jesus.

Can Come Upon Us

Danger can come upon us any day that we need the Lord's protection from our head down to our feet.

Sickness can come upon us and get us down, but the Lord will lift us up to see his goodness all around us.

Trouble can come upon us, but Jesus can give us peace that cannot be moved from the north, south, west and east.

Jesus Christ is Lord of Lords and King of Kings, beyond anything that can come upon us even in a dream that can come true.

The world can come upon us with lies that God's holy word can erase from our minds and fill our eyes with the truth of Jesus, who's alive forever and ever in heaven on high.

Our sins can come upon us, but Jesus will give us a victory over them.

Carry Us Through

O Lord, You have to carry us through the day that can move slow or rush by us and go away.

O Lord, You have to carry us through our minds that won't be right without you in it all the time.

You, Lord Jesus, have to carry us through our hearts for us to feel good, even in our trials.

It is good for us to hold onto You, O Lord, who have to carry us through our prayers.

We always trust You to answer our prayers in Your time that we must wait on.

Lord Jesus, You have to carry us so we can have patience instead of trying to get things in a hurry that can bury us in an early grave.

O Lord, You have to carry us through our selfishness day after day so we can choose to repent of our sins to be saved.

You have to carry us through our fears and our tears when You, O Lord, can give us cheer.

Can't Add To and Take Out

We can write a poem and add words to fit and take out words from it to fit into a song.

We can't add words to the Bible or take out any words from the Bible. It is always reliable to tell us the truth about God the Father, Son and Holy Ghost.

We can write a book for many folks to read and stay on their minds, but we can't add to and take out any words from the Bible.

You and I can read about the holy angels and fallen angels who are higher than man.

We can read in the Bible and learn how man and woman fell into sin.

We can read in the Bible about God's son, Jesus Christ, and how he came to be on the cross.

We can't add to or take out the cost that Jesus paid for you and me to be saved in Him.

The Bible says that until we go to the grave we can't add to or take out any word from the Bible in any way.

We Must Wait

If the weather is bad, we must wait on it to be good on another day.

We must wait on the Lord to work out our problems, which he will do without a doubt.

If we wait on Jesus, who waits on you and me to give Him all of our hearts, He will set us free from our selfish ways that can get us in trouble.

We must wait on the Lord to bless us and secure our trust in Him, who blesses the sun to rise and set.

We must wait on dreams to come to us in our sleep, as we wait on the Lord to meet us and plant our feet on his holy ground.

We must wait to reach up to spiritual heights and we must wait to know the deep things of the Lord, who waits on his one lost sheep.

Just Imagine

Just imagine in the new heaven and in the new earth we will always have something to do for Jesus who so first loved us.

We can just imagine for only right now that we must be saved in Jesus Christ, whose holy ground is stretched out from heaven to earth and throughout the universe.

We can just imagine with a shout for joy in the Lord, who created all thing without a doubt.

We can just imagine being with our Lord Jesus Christ, who lives forever and ever.

He is eternal life that the holy angels and other worlds do proclaim.

So many people in this sinful world will deny Jesus' holy name.

All the saints can just imagine to go to heaven one day with Jesus, who is making streets of pure gold.

We can just imagine to walking those streets upon our feet.

If We Try to Work Our Way

If we try to work our way to be saved, we would have no faith in Jesus who gave up his life on the cross and rose from the grave to save our souls.

We can't expect to receive eternal life if we try to work our way to heaven.

God would see no favor in our righteousness; it would be like filthy rags to God, who forever knows that we can't brag about salvation with our works.

We won't please God unless we believe in his Son, Jesus Christ, whose ministry work is forever worthy above our works.

Our works can't save anyone in the church or out of the church.

Jesus wants to save everyone who has to work out their own soul's salvation to be saved in Jesus who is about to come back one day soon.

Faith and believing people will be pure if we love Jesus Christ like we should so we will be saved in him real good.

In the Big Picture

Jesus is in the big picture that the devil can't steal.

No matter how many times he tries, he will fail.

Jesus didn't leave us out of the big picture that looks so beautiful in God's love.

The big picture has some dust of death on it that Jesus will blow off with his breath of life.

One day, when He comes back again, he will give eternal life to all who are saved from their sins.

Only those who are saved will be in the big picture that Jesus bought with his life on the cross to pay our price.

In the big picture the devil can't afford to ever buy us, thanks to Jesus Christ our Savior and Lord.

In the Sunset of Time

We are living in the sunset of time.

It is getting dark upon grace that will not shine like the sun.

As we get closer and closer to Jesus Christ coming back again, it is the sunset of time.

You and I are living during these last days on earth, and time is setting like the sun.

Jesus and all of his angels will appear as Jesus raises the righteous dead to eternal life and the righteous living to immortality in this dark land of sin.

Jesus will one day bring an end to this sinful world

In the sunset of time, the sun will rise again in heaven above, where all the saints will enjoy God's everlasting love.

The Activities of Life

The activities of life are a gift from the Lord who lives forever, loves and uplifts.

We're all moving around here and there, whether being wise or being a fool.

Jesus owns them both in the activities of life that are corrupt with sin.

Jesus Christ is coming back again to raise the righteous dead to eternal life with the righteous living.

Because Jesus paid the price to allow the activities of life to go on and for souls to be saved.

You and I are so blessed to still be alive in the activities of life that God holds in his eternal hands.

Our hands can hold sorrow, sickness and death for us to see no tomorrow.

The activities of life are a gift from the Lord, who lives forever loves and uplifts.

Love Keeps Me Going

Love keeps me going through the thick and thin.

Love gets me through in my life.

Love keeps me going strong from day to day.

I long for love that God gives to me the most.

Because God is love from coast to coast.

God so loved the world that he sent us his only begotten son for you and me.

See His love all around this world.

Love keeps me going up and down.

My life keeps me going through the storms.

God's love will keep me going so I can one day go to heaven above.

Is With Oneself

Most battles are fought with oneself each and everyday.

Oneself can't be anyone else.

The greatest honesty is to be honest with oneself.

God can help us to see the truth about oneself who can have the most control over oneself from head to toes.

Jesus can use us for his glory.

Oneself has the greatest story to tell about oneself who is nothing good without Jesus, whose hands and feet were nailed in the wood of a cross to save me from my sins.

You can't save yourself.

Oneself can be my worst enemy day after day, if I don't love and obey Jesus Christ every day.

I have to work out my own soul's salvation in my life.

That is with oneself making good or bad choices to be in a battle with oneself for only Jesus to set free.

Life is Like

Life is like the wind that blows.

We don't know what direction life will blow us on any day.

Life is like leaves falling off of a tree onto the ground to dry up in the fall season.

Life is like the green grass turning brown from the scorching heat from the sun shining all around you and me.

Life owes nothing to us.

We can take life for a hit and run like driving away in a car after hitting someone.

We can do this to Jesus Christ if you and I don't live our lives day after day doing God's will.

Life is like eating a good and healthy meal that is good for us to live a long, healthy life.

This is a gift from our Lord and Savior Jesus Christ.

Over the Years

Over the years you have made me to be a lot stronger in you, O Lord, who I don't see but surely believe in.

You are the reason that I am still alive today to see the seasons.

Being a blessing from you who has shown mercy on me over the years that have flown by me like a bird in the sky, hovering over the years that have passed by me so fast.

I am so blessed to have eyes to see and have strength in my body to move around here and there over the years to prove that You, my Lord and Savior Jesus Christ, are not finished with me yet.

Only You, O Lord, can keep my life ticking like a clock.

In Our Lives

Jesus can make the sun to shine in our lives.

Jesus is always on time to bless us.

Jesus can make the flowers bloom in our lives.

The rain showers of Jesus can refresh and cleanse with his love.

Jesus can make the stars from heaven above sparkle so bright in our lives that need more of Jesus each and every day.

Jesus can make a door open in our lives that no one can close except the Lord.

Jesus Christ can make the darkness of sin break its chain in our lives if we come into His holy-holy sanctuary and worship Him with all of our hearts, minds and soul yielding to his call.

I Am Rich

I am rich to be alive because of Jesus who has made me rich in living with good health to do good things. I am rich with a mind to think on my Lord Jesus Christ, whose always on time to make a way out of no way for me.

I am rich with contentment as I bow down on my knees unto the Lord, who has made me rich with a free will to choose right from wrong day by day.

I am rich to be real and talk with good sense and do right in Jesus' name.

I am rich in being saved and having the Holy Ghost to live in me day after day.

I can be rich in death for being saved in Jesus Christ, who gave up his life to save me from the poverty of my sins.

Life is About

Life is not about being great.

Life is about being humble before the Lord day after day.

Life is not about getting rich.

Life is about being spiritually rich in Jesus Christ, who left all the riches in heaven to become poor on earth and save poor souls so they get spiritually rich in the Lord God of heaven and earth.

Life is not about being a hero.

Life is about knowing that Jesus is all-powerful and can go where no man can — to the end of the universe.

Life is not about being on top of the ladder and being the first to cross over the finish line.

Life is about Jesus Christ saving us from our sins.

Life is not about leaning to our own ways of doing things.

Life is about living for Jesus Christ the King of Kings.

This World is Not My Home

This world is not my home.

This world oppresses me with lies and deceptions day after day.

I can see that this world is not my home and I don't want it to be my home because I love Jesus Christ and want to go with him to heaven when he comes back again full of everlasting power and the glory of eternal life. He gives this to me.

This world is not my home for me to live in it without Jesus in my life.

This sinful world loves to oppress us with its selfish ways that will surely do you and me wrong and has done me so wrong since the day that I was born.

Jesus is with me in every way for me to see this day.

This world is not my home to put my trust in.

This world will leave me all alone to be lost and die in my sins that Jesus gave up his life and rose from the grave to save me from.

This world is not my home day after day.

This world will oppress me with its greed and lust for power every second, minute and hour.

This world's temporary things are bitter and sour to my soul.

Energize My Life

Thinking about You, O Lord, energizes my life to a wide awakening.

That is so nice of You, O Lord, to open my mind up to Your spiritual things flowing all through my life.

O Lord, You energize me from day to day.

By doing Your will, my Lord Jesus Christ will stay close to my heart.

Praying to You, O Lord, will energize my life as well.

Obeying You so real, O Lord, energizes my life for me to feel so good.

I call on Your holy and precious name that energizes my life and eases my pain.

You keep me going strong in You, my Lord.

You always know how to give good rewards.

The Grass is Greener in Jesus

The grass is greener in Jesus who will keep the grass greener in our life.

If you and I will love and obey Jesus Christ, the grass will always be greener in our lives.

We need to be loving Jesus and keeping his golden rules, even when the rain, snow, and dew falls down on the grass on the ground — even where the green grass can turn brown.

In this world the grass is not always greener, and Jesus is the answer each and every day.

Jesus has no brown grass in his truth and grace.

The grass is greener in Jesus who can save our souls from being lost in the brown grass of the devil, whose grass will dry up fast and will only appear to look green but won't last.

Mysterious As

Mysterious as the full white moon glowing in the night is God who can work in mysterious ways to reveal the light of his truth to people who don't know all the truth of his holy word.

Mysterious as an empty boat on the ocean waters is God who can work in mysterious ways for many souls to come into the church and worship his only begotten son, Jesus Christ.

Jesus was a mysterious sinless man to many people who knew that He was different from anyone they'd ever seen, as they got healed of their sickness by the King of Kings.

Mysterious as a deep forest filled with trees is God who can work in mysterious ways that we don't see but can surely be blessed by God who is so good to you and me.

God has some mysterious ways of dealing with us.

Only God knows so well that we can trust Him to show us our mysterious ways under the sunlight rays.

You Are Every Good Thing

My Lord and Savior Jesus Christ, You are every good thing in this life and in the after life to come to me.

I am saved in You, O Lord, who sets me free with your truth that is eternal.

You are every good thing from the sin bearer to the King of Kings and beyond.

My new birth in you, my Lord Jesus, is every good thing, even the good things that I've never seen.

My life on earth is too short for me to see all the good things that overflow the heavens.

I call on Your good holy name, O Lord, as I know You make good things to exist everyday in a world of many mean and hateful people.

You, O Lord, also give good things to people, even though they don't do your will.

You, O Lord, are every good thing to fulfill Your holy law that is always good.

Some Things We Must Overlook

Some things we must overlook and not get hooked on.

Our minds don't need to dwell on the things that can offend us like a slap in the face and a stomp on the hand.

Jesus will never do us wrong. He wants us to always feel good about doing His holy will.

That is something to never overlook each and every day.

There are some things that we must overlook to stay positive in a world of so many selfish people who are so self-absorbed and only concerned with themselves.

They do wrong things, even in the church where you and I must overlook them sometimes if it's not so bad.

Some things that people do are offensive.

We all must bow down on our knees unto Jesus, who we all offend with our sins He always sees.

Shines Over

The sunlight shines over you and me, who are so blessed to see the sun shining so very free.

Over you and me, the full white moonlight glows all night long while we sleep and dream away into the morning of another day.

The streetlights will sleep away and wake up in the night to shine over you and me, who have sins to repent unto Jesus Christ who shines over our souls.

He saves us in His light of truth and grace that angels behold, while many sinners die young and go to the grave below.

I Thank You for Using Me

O Lord, I thank You for using me who has flaws that can be sharp as a bear's claws.

O Lord, I thank You for using me who has bad habits that stick to me like glue no matter where I am.

O Lord, I thank You for using me who doesn't always talk right and do right on my spiritual walk.

O Lord, I thank You for using me who has sins to confess and repent unto you.

O Lord, I thank You for using me who wants to love you and obey You each and every day.

O Lord, You will always help me to do your holy will for as long as I want to be used by you who will never do me wrong.

If it's Not in God's Word

Whatever someone says, if it's not in line with God's word, it's not true at any time of the day and night.'

It's not easy to think when someone is talking to you and me and they talk, talk and talk away.

If it's not according to God's holy word, then what they say is not true — no matter how we dress it up.

Some talking can sound good, even in the church where sin can abound to blind people's eyes to not see their pride, jealousy and selfishness taking them on a destructive ride to the devil's dead end road.

Many church folks will talk words of no Bible truth to load you and me down with lies in their talk about religion. But they are crippled and have no holy talk.

Hold Onto

A tree can hold onto its roots, but a tree has no living soul to be free to make choices day after day.

The grass will hold onto the ground that's way below the sun, moon and stars that will hold onto the universe.

We have a living soul to hold onto Jesus Christ who holds all existence in place.

The fall, winter, spring and summer hold onto the seasons.

We have a living soul to hold onto Jesus' reason to let us live another day, week, month and year.

We can hold onto the choices that we make to be so clear to Jesus who we can always hold onto so dear.

We are living souls for Jesus to save from being lost like a boat being lost off its course.

Jesus is Forever and Ever

Mountains are high to reach the sky.

Jesus is forever and ever in heaven on high above the valleys that are deep and the oceans that are deep.

They cannot be deeper that the devotion of Jesus' love that is forever and ever deep.

We have dreams in our sleep, but life is real to live, doing right or wrong to be produced into so many songs.

Jesus Christ our Lord of Lords and King of Kings is forever and ever real beyond the sunlight beams up in heaven where mortal eyes never seen.

Jesus sits on His holy throne with his Heavenly Father, God, who loves his son, Jesus, with all of His heart.

Can Come and Go

Romantic love can come and go far to a desolate place like a falling star.

Only the Lord knows where it has fallen.

Money can come and go to an empty checking account that you and I can get if we overspend.

The Lord is not pleased with us doing this, regardless of the hours that we work on our time clock in this world where a good reputation can come and go, we can do something bad that no words can cover up from the Lord no matter what we say.

God's love will come and go around the world day after day.

God's love is forever true in every way.

Feelings can come and go but God's word will never change.

God will tell us about our sins.

Youth can come and go to old age in the end.

Paradise in You

If you have Jesus in you, you have paradise in you because Jesus Christ is paradise to you and me if we are saved in Jesus through his paradise grace.

Jesus is truth and grace being more beautiful than any paradise on earth.

Jesus Christ our Lord once lived on earth with His paradise presence that calmed the storm.

Jesus spoke to it to not harm His disciples in the boat

We church folks have paradise in us for believing in Jesus who loves our souls to repent and live a renewed life in Him.

He is the living paradise for no sin to exist when paradise on earth have sins of men.

A Lot of People

A lot of people will pray to You, O Lord, but they won't read your holy word day after day.

A lot of people will call on Your holy name, O Lord, but they won't love you who has no blame or any trace of sin.

Every human being has it in their sinful nature to not always pass Your test.

A lot of people will do good things in Your name, O Lord, but they won't obey you who cleanses us of our sins.

A lot of people won't confess and repent of their sins at all but will say that they love You and believe that it's true.

O Lord, a lot of people will disobey and believe that it doesn't matter to You, Lord Jesus, who knows that a lot of people are playing church twenty-four hours around the clock.

I Need To

I need to love and obey the Lord, who knows how to open and shut doors, always on time.

I need to love my neighbors as I love myself, who I can shove away from the Lord if I don't do God's will.

I always need to do everyday that is God-sent to me.

I need to give God the glory and praise for as long as I live.

I need to believe in God's son, Jesus Christ, and need to live my life for Him every day and every night.

I need to have faith in Jesus, who lives forever above the sky.

I need to deny myself and give Jesus a try.

I need to live by God's holy word because Jesus is the living word from heaven on high.

It's Not Me

It's not me who can think right, for it's the Lord who gives me the right thoughts to think on all through the day.

It's not me to say the right words, when it's the Lord who gives me the right words to say day in and day out.

It's not me who can do right, for it's the Lord who helps me to do right and to be on one accord with my brothers and sisters in His holy name. He makes me to be more and more like him for others to see.

It's not me who can live right, when it's the Lord who lives in me and makes me live right according to His holy will.

It's not me whose will is tarnished in sin, when it's the Lord who has no sin and gets me through the thick and thin.

My Own Heart

I do not always know my own heart, so how can I know anyone else's heart?

Hearts are filled with the unknown to me, but not to God, who always knows how to talk to my heart even when my thoughts are infested with sin.

Sin can get in my mind, even when I am in the church.

I need Jesus Christ to help me to see the devil's lies and deceptions are not in line with God's word and discourage me and make me weak in my heart.

You, my Lord Jesus, always know too well all through my life that I don't always know my own heart.

You, O Lord, always do my heart good.

I don't have a clue about what's in someone else's heart, but I do know Jesus can renew.

It's Always Good

It's always good for you and me to love our neighbors every day. That is the greatest gospel labor.

It's always good for you and me to help our neighbors who need it.

It's always good to have faith in the Lord Jesus Christ, who is always so good to us and blesses our lives more abundantly for trusting and obeying Him every day.

It's always good to treat our neighbors right in every way possible in God's holy sight.

It's always good for God to watch over our souls as we try to always love our neighbors and do them no evil in every neighborhood.

It Doesn't Take Much

It's doesn't take much to think wrong thoughts. They can enter into our minds to not exhort the Lord.

It doesn't take much to talk wrong and ruin our relationships and daily walk with the Lord.

He always knows that it doesn't take much for you and me to make a mistake on any day.

It also doesn't take much for us to doubt the Lord, who knows that we can lose touch with trusting him when disappointment crushes our spirits that the Lord can heal.

The Lord will let us know that it doesn't take much for Him to save our souls if we confess and repent, no matter if we are young or old.

Are You and I Ready?

Many women want a husband and many men want a wife.

They are not ready for the ups and downs in life that a marriage can bring on.

This is so clear to see in a world where many people want to get married but can't be committed to go through what a marriage has to put on the table.

In the church are you and I ready to be married to Jesus Christ?

We must suffer for His holy name's sake and go through the ups and downs on our Christian walk.

This is the only way for us to know that we are faithful unto Him, who is the husband of the church.

He won't put more on us than what we can bear.

When are we ready to work out our own soul's salvation, that will keep us spiritually alert in the church.

Burdens Will Fly Away

Burdens will fly away when the truth is spoken and lived to set you and me free from deception that can bind us for so very long.

Jesus is so merciful to make our burdens fly away and go to a place of no return, to ease our minds and give us peace.

This is especially helpful during a time of ignorance that can bring you and me down.

Even on God's holy ground, sin can snoop around and wear you and me out.

Jesus will step in and set us free with the truth that sin hates to see.

Jesus will be setting us free from our burdens that will fly away when you and I confess and repent of our sins Jesus always sees deceiving you and me.

There is a Good Kind of Fear

There is a good kind of fear and that is to fear God.

We do this by keeping His commandments deep within our hearts

Fearing God won't cause you and me to run and hide away from what is good.

We can fear what man can do to us if we don't fear God and put our trust in Him from day to day.

Many people live in the wrong kind of fear that will give them stress.

That can happen to you and me if we don't fear God who set us free from the wrong kind of fear.

Fearing Him is a good kind of fear that the world needs to see.

Short of Your Glory

If it was always easy for me to do everything that you say

O Lord then I wouldn't fall short of your glory day after day

When I will fall short of your glory in some kind of seen

And unseen way that I will not do everything

Right all the time that I will not say everything right for me

To fall short of your glory that I truly see

Regardless of your holy word being preached to me to set me free

From lies far from your truth that my own righteousness can't live

Up to for me to fall short of your glory O Lord that your holy will is perfect and beyond my will that can do You so wrong.

No matter how long that I have been in the church where I can be a storm.

In your eyesight O Lord for not doing all that you say for me to fall.

Short of your glory when my all is not good enough to save me in all

Of your glory that I will fall short of whether if I am great or small

Is the Free Will Choice a Wrong Thing?

Is the free will choice a wrong thing when we can choose to do wrong?

It seems in our daily living that we can live to choose what we want to say and what we want to do.

If the free will choice is a wrong thing to do, then God would have destroyed this world a long time ago to get rid of all this sin that we commit against Him because of our wrong choice that he sees.

God did no wrong to give us all the free will choice out of His love for us, so we would love him so real.

Our free will doesn't mean the devil can control you and me.

We have to choose our destiny so aware or not aware upon the land.

Looking Out for Me

I thank You, O Lord, for looking out for me.

You always know what I need, even when I don't always see.

I thank You, O Lord, for looking out for me, who can do You more wrong than right when I don't trust You like I need to every day and every night.

I thank You, Lord Jesus, for always looking out for me, even when I don't always look out for You.

I can doubt Your love and disobey You even when I'm aware of what I do.

I am so guilty in Your eyes that see all of my lies.

I am so thankful unto You, my Lord Jesus Christ, for looking out for me when I don't deserve it all of my life.

Strong Love

Couples who stick together through thick and thin surely have a strong love that can hold together to the end of their lives.

It takes a strong love to mend a broken heart and cause it to love again in a world where strong love is hardly seen.

From day to day a lot of things are going on making us need strong love.

It takes God's strong love to get us beyond and above our fears and worries.

You and I can give our worries to the Lord, who gives us his strong love that will always lift us up when we fall down in sin.

Love is stronger than hate, no matter where it dwells.

The Lord Will Wait for Us

A second won't wait for us to say something right or wrong.

A minute won't wait for you and me to do something right or wrong. In that minute, we may not have a clue about how we will choose or what to do.

An hour won't wait for us to give or not give our hearts to the Lord.

It can be too late to give him our hearts when the hours of the day come to an end.

Time won't wait for us to trust the Lord, but the Lord will wait for us to choose our destiny before we return to the dust of the earth.

We can wait for the Lord to work out every bad situation that we put ourselves in.

O Lord, You Use

O Lord, You use messed up people who have sins to confess and repent of unto you.

My Lord, You use flawed people to spread your gospel to all the world, telling that being messed up in sin is to fall short of your glory.

O Lord, You use wretched people to win souls unto You, who will one day put an end to all sin.

You, O Lord, love to save a sinner like me, and You give me Your amazing grace every day.

You, Lord Jesus, use peculiar people as a chosen generation of priesthood to be set free from being lost in this world that the saints do see.

Another Moment

Another moment is not promised to you and me.

We could die any moment. That, I truly see.

My life could be taken away from me so fast that I could truly be dead, if Jesus was to pass me by at my last breath.

I may not receive another moment to live. This moment is all that I have to hold onto.

Being saved in Jesus can give me another moment to thank Him for sparing my life to live and experience more and more of his mercy and grace.

I have another moment during which I should say that Jesus Christ is Lord every moment of the day.

On the Outside and the Inside

A lot of women are beautiful on the outside and broken on the inside.

A lot of men are strong on the outside and broken on the inside, no matter if their hands can crush you and me.

We can look put well together on the outside and be broken on the inside, like the bad weather breaking up things here and there in its path.

The Lord can always fix a broken heart day by day.

We need to pray unto the Lord and give our hearts to Him.

Our outward appearances can be deceiving, but not to God.

He's not so concerned about what's on the outside, but He is most certainly concerned about us being broken up in our sins on the inside.

Jesus Says

Many church folks will say to Jesus, "I preach in your name."

Jesus says to them, "You don't live what you say. You're playing a game with your soul's salvation." Many church folks will say, "I sing songs in Your name."

Jesus says, "You do things your way and not My way, which is My will for you each and every day."

Many church folks will say, "Jesus, I do good deeds in Your name."

Jesus says, "You do them with the wrong motives and are no friend to Me, who will always be a good friend."

Jesus says, "Depart from me. I never knew you who didn't love Me."

Jesus says, "You didn't teach all of My truth from your heart and were not convinced and converted in the eyes of God."

Many church folks will say, "I am saved in Jesus' name."

Jesus says, "You are lost, because you trample over My grace."

We Can Be Doubtful

We can be doubtful about talking to one another, and be doubtful about trust.

Brothers and sisters in the Lord should never doubt to talk to or doubt to trust.

Jesus is always there for you and me to lean on in every way.

We can put all of our insecurities in Jesus, and He will pick us up when we fall.

We can doubt that our church brothers and sisters may not always be there for us because they have some real hard issues in their lives.

Only Jesus can fix these issues.

We can be so broken in doubting Jesus more than a little bit, and we can also be doubtful about one another, especially when things are not going well in our lives.

We should never doubt that Jesus is our best friend.

Close to Jesus

You and I can always get close to Jesus.

He will let us get close to Him no matter what we go through in our lives.

There are many church folks who wouldn't let us get close to them.

They may be soaked down in being broken and push you and me away.

Jesus will never do that to you and me on any day.

We can get close to Jesus Christ. He won't put up a wall to separate Himself from us.

We can always look forward to getting to know Jesus more and more.

Many church folks will avoid even looking or talking to you and me.

The Lord will never avoid us and is always available to talk.

It's a Miracle

It's a miracle to be healed from a sickness, to restore good health.

So many are dying so young, and lay on their deathbeds.

Death can come to you and me at any time — it's unpredictable.

It's a miracle to get old in this dying world.

We don't know how long our lives will last.

Jesus can prolong our years, regardless of our sins.

It's a miracle to receive the gift of God's grace upon you and me.

Jesus wants to save us.

It's a miracle to still be alive to especially live unto the Lord.

If There Was No Law

If there was no law, then there would be no prisons to lock up criminals.

No one would know right from wrong when we need moral living every day.

The law stands for something good, like the Bible says about God's law.

We all do break God's Law in some kind of way every day, because we all were born in sin and that breaks God's law.

If there was no law, there would be no good morals at all to hold onto.

God's law is His character for you and me to know.

God's law is His love to all the world through his son, Jesus Christ, who was a sinless man who never broke God's law in his life on earth. Jesus was the law wrapped up in the flesh.

Be Still

Be still, look up in the sky and see God's glory going down through the history of the Bible stories.

Be still, listen and hear the Lord's voice speaking to us in nature that is on one accord.

When we are making strife we're not being of the Lord, who will be still and hear our prayers if we are doing God's holy will from the bottom of our hearts.

We need to be still and let Jesus Christ come in and be in control of our lives day after day.

You and I need to be still and see the Lord working things out for us so very real.

We need to be still and love and obey Jesus every day that we live.

Only Once in a Lifetime

There are people who we will see only once in a lifetime.

There are people who we will talk to only once under the sunshine.

We can go here and there and see people who we've never seen before as they pass us by going through life's ups and downs.

Everyone can grab a-hold of God's salvation through his son, Jesus Christ.

Time owes Him every second, minute and hour.

You and I need to treasure our time here on earth.

It's time to be all about living for Jesus.

There are many people who we will have a good or bad effect on only once in a lifetime.

We will see some people only once and then they are gone to where only God knows to save their souls. The Lord is always fair and saves all who believe in Him.

The Lord will come around us a lot more than once in a lifetime. That, we can surely trust.

Believing in Jesus

There is nothing better than believing in Jesus Christ.

We can believe He'll make a way out of no way in this life on earth.

There is nothing better than believing in Jesus.

We can believe that He will never be deceiving in any kind of way.

There is nothing better than believing in Jesus.

We can believe He will never tell us to take a hike when we need him.

We can believe in Jesus to forgive us and cleanse us of our sins that he took on for us on the cross.

There is nothing better than believing in Jesus.

We can believe He cares about saving our souls and taking us to heaven with Him one day.

There is nothing better than believing in Jesus, just like the Bible says.

It's a Blessing

It's a blessing to have this freedom to worship You, Lord Jesus, on your holy Sabbath day of rest.

It will always do my mind and body good to come into Your holy sanctuary and give You, O Lord, all the glory and praise that You deserve.

Every man, woman, boy and girl needs to know that it's a blessing to know the truth of Your holy word.

O Lord, You will go with me to the end of my life that I want to live doing Your holy will.

It's a blessing that gives me peace of mind every day of the week.

Your word is health to my bones, from my head to my feet.

It's a blessing to meet with You, O Lord, on Your holy Sabbath day of rest that no one should avoid.

You and I Don't Need

You and I don't need a college degree to know how to treat people right.

We go here and there, and you and I don't need to be known to love people.

We don't always see the need to pray for everyone to give their hearts to the one and only true living God.

You and I don't need to say one word about who we are to people who will see Jesus living in us, if we are born again in Jesus Christ, who doesn't need you or me, but we need Him every day.

We don't need to be like the people of the world who strive to be great when we need to be humble.

Jesus is the greatest of the great for doing His heavenly Father's holy will.

Jesus lived on earth without sin to fulfill His mission to save us.

Will Always Be Up Against Something

We will always be up against something for being a Christian every day.

The Lord is with us to help us get through what we go through for His holy name's sake.

The devil sees to it there is hate every day.

We will always be up against something that will come our way.

We need to put our trust in Jesus, who won't delay His help, if we are born again in Jesus Christ, who doesn't need you or me.

If we don't give it to Jesus Christ, who was always up against something when He lived his life on earth to be our Lord, then our souls will be lost to our Lord and Savior who paid our price.

Can Seem to be Forever

A very bad storm can seem to be forever around, high up in the sky before it touches down on the ground.

It can seem to be forever present all around.

Some hard times can seem to be forever upon us, and we may not see things getting better in our lives.

It can seem to be forever standing still when nothing good is going on in our lives.

We need Jesus Christ in our lives to cleanse us of our sins that will cause us to be to forever lost if we don't make Jesus our choice.

We have to choose to be forever with him one day.

It can seem to be to be forever far away before we get to see Jesus on the clouds of glory.

Sin can seem to be forever close to us, before we get to see Jesus one day.

Our Ways Can

Our ways can move like the clouds moving across the sky

The Lord's ways can move in a mysterious way in heaven on high and on earth.

We can move here and there and it can seem like we're going nowhere.

As the clouds move across the sky so peacefully and go to another place in the sky, things clear up.

Our ways that can move to a place for only Jesus Christ to know and move our ways out of His way.

Our lives can get renewed so we can be saved and one day meet Jesus on the clouds of glory.

Then we will be full of grace from God, who created the clouds to move across the sky.

We Can Create Our Own Tornado

We can create our own tornado of disappointment if we put our trust in ourselves.

We can get blown down and become scraps of failure.

We can create our own tornado of heartaches if we don't wait on the Lord whose love will never fail us.

We can create our own tornado of trouble if we take things into our own hands.

We're bound to fail without the Lord's help. He knows how to send the tornados away.

In the Lord, we won't get blown down by our own mistakes.

We can make our own tornado of not doing what the Bible says.

Jesus can calm the storm.

We can create our own tornado of doubting what Jesus can do to bless our hands.

Holding onto Him and doing his will doesn't bring tornados down upon the land.

Let's Be Real

Let's be real, we will fall short of the glory of God in some kind of way.

We can believe that our hearts are always right with God, but we can be in some kind of denial and not be real.

God is always on time to wake us up to see the truth that is always real.

It sets us free from lies that we can tell to ourselves to feel good when we're not right in the Lord's holy eyesight.

We will fall short, whether it's in what we say or what we do.

For us to be real is to confess and repent of our sins unto the Lord Jesus Christ.

He is always so real and gives us many chances to surrender our lives unto him who paid our price.

All We Can Do

All we can do is to live one day at a time and try to do the best we can do under the sun that shines.

All around there is no control over what a day will bring us.

All we can do is hold onto Jesus in every way.

That, we need to do, day after day.

All we can do is the best that we can, beyond the mistakes that you and I make.

Jesus will suffer long with us because he knows that we will not always fully trust Him who can do all things.

We can doubt He will give us all that we need.

Even this day, all we can do is try our best to do good.

In life we can only live once in this world.

The best thing we can do is to do God's holy will. It's the best thing that can happen to me and you.

The Lord Can Use Anybody

The Lord can use anybody.

There is no big you and little me in his eyesight that sees all people to be equal.

The Lord can use anybody to do His holy will because God has given us all a free will to hear His voice and obey his call.

The Lord can use you and me to be witnesses for Him.

The Lord loves with an everlasting love that you and I need to give back to Him who can set us free from feeling like we are nobody for Him to use.

The Lord can use anybody who wants to be used by Him.

He can bring us through anything, even when we don't have a clue.

The Church is Not Hollywood

The church is not Hollywood where you and I can be a star.

Some people act like they are Hollywood in the church.

Jesus Christ is the head of the church to save souls and renew our lives.

To live and do God's will is not like Hollywood.

In this church it's always a good thing to humble ourselves and show a good example to Hollywood.

We surely know that Jesus is the bright and morning star, shining God's love, truth, humility and grace in our hearts.

The Lord is not pleased with any play-acting that Hollywood will do.

God is a Miracle

God is a miracle that is all around us every day and every night.

God is a miracle above what the Bible says about God.

God is a miracle all through the heavens and earth.

God's blessings are a miracle that God gives to us who need to do God's will, being his ten golden rules to keep so real.

God is the miracle of miracles that we don't see because of our sinful nature not being free from sinning against God, whose only begotten Son is a miracle to save us from our sins.

God can do miracles in his Son's name.

God can save sinners and give us a new heart.

Love is Thicker

Love is thicker than any blood kin, because it's love that brings people together through the thick and thin.

The life that we live is to love and not hate our fellow man.

Love is thicker than blood all across the land where blood kin can fuss and fight with one another.

The mother and father and sister and the brother can be against each other.

You and I can love a friend who's not a blood kin who can be against you and me like Cain was against his brother Abel.

He killed him because God had showed him favor for Abel's sacrifice unto Him.

God is love that is thicker than any blood kin being of any race and creed.

Love can help to overcome anything because love is thicker than any blood kin under the sun.

O Lord Help Me

O Lord, help me to talk right and do right because I don't want to run anyone out of the church.

I need to keep my eyes on you, my Lord, who I need to help me to love everyone inside and outside the church.

I need you from morning 'til night.

I want to do your holy will, O Lord, who is real to help me get filled with Your Holy Spirit who tells me the truth about You.

You are there for me when I need you, O Lord, to help me to humble myself and give You all the glory that You deserve.

I deserve to fall so low down into guilt and shame for not always giving my all to You, my Lord Jesus Christ, who blesses me day after day.

I need you to help me to pray unto You.

The Heart

The heart can be a confusing thing, for only God to always understand it so as it seems.

The heart can be a deadly thing for only God to always see the evil in the heart day by day.

The heart can be an unpredictable thing for only God to always predict it and surely bring the heart out of its movable ways because the heart can be here and there.

Only God always knows where it's at and where it's going to day after day.

The heart can love God, who always knows how much love to give from heaven above.

The heart that loves Jesus will have more life than every heartbeat in me and you.

I Am So Glad

I am so glad that You, O Lord, will talk to me down on my level.

You will always walk with me through my trials.

I am so glad that You, my Lord, understand me and go with me to the deep thoughts in my mind.

I am so glad that you dwell in me so on time.

You, O Lord, lift me up to shine in your love.

I am so glad that You love me and will never leave me or forsake me through my bad days.

I am so glad to follow You today.

You, O Lord, have control over my today and tomorrow, like You did in my yesterdays.

We All Have

We all have some things in common.

We all can feel happy and sad and we all can get real sick.

We all can feel pain and we all can stumble and fall down.

We all can call our Lord's holy name and feel relieved of our burdens.

We all can believe that Jesus Christ is Lord and the light of the world.

We all can love or not love Jesus because we all have something in common.

We all were born in sin, except for Jesus, who has some things in common with us.

Jesus felt what we all feel and we can trust Him because he overcame all that we feel from dust 'til dawn.

Doing My Own Thing

Doing my own thing has gotten me into trouble more than a few times as I go through life.

I have truly learned that doing my own thing has earned me disappointments and heartaches.

So I have decided to do the things that Jesus would have me to do, instead.

I love doing what Jesus wants me to do, beyond doing my own thing that got me nowhere in life except being alone in my misery.

The Lord brought me out of that misery when I decided to do things His way so He could save me from my sins.

Spreading the Gospel

Spreading the gospel of Jesus Christ is not about making money; it is about renewing a life to live for Jesus.

A sermon and a gospel song are both about winning souls unto Jesus, who does no wrong to you and me who can be set free in the truth of His gospel.

Jesus Christ will always love us to the end of our lives.

It will take a lifetime to spread the gospel of Jesus Christ.

It will take us until we are dead in our graves.

Spreading the gospel of Jesus Christ is not about making a name for you or me, even though a lot of people are doing that and causing souls to be lost around the clock.

What it takes is spreading the gospel of Jesus Christ on every street block, road and trail around the world where Jesus has His flock.

The Most Powerful Thing on Earth

The most powerful thing on earth is the free will choice.

It is the first thing we do every day.

You and I can choose to love or hate so free, because the most powerful thing on earth is the free will choice that God gives to us all.

We have to choose so real from sunrise to sunset to sunrise under the sky.

The devil can't take away our free will choice with his lies.

We can choose or not to choose to believe in anything when we can choose to believe in Jesus Christ who we can see in His holy word that we can choose to read.

The devil can't make us do anything against our free will.

We can make the free will choice for our better or our worse.

The Higher Up

The higher up we go, the more we need to keep ourselves humble unto the Lord.

He should be first in our lives.

We can't live exalting ourselves like many selfish people.

Doing that will make us fall down and do bad things.

The higher up we rise, the more sins we need to confess and repent of unto the Lord who is forever high above us.

This is when we need Jesus like never before.

We go up higher to fall down in sin if we don't give Jesus Christ all the glory and praise.

He is the one who takes us up higher in life.

We must not glorify self.

Jesus Christ, our Lord, blesses us with the price he paid for our sins with his life.

Who is All

I don't know anything, O Lord, when it comes to You, who is all-knowing beyond and below the great blue sky.

I don't see anything when it comes to You, O Lord, who is all-seeing from eternity to eternity.

I can't do anything, O Lord, who is all-doing in heaven and on earth.

Your love soars through all existence.

You, O Lord, are before and after life here on earth.

I don't hear anything when it comes to You, O Lord, who is all-hearing near and afar across the universe.

You, O Lord, are dear to me, who is nothing when it comes to you who is all cheer.

Going Through the Motions of Life

There was a time when I was going through the motions of life.

I didn't give any glory and praise to my Lord Jesus Christ, who brought me through the motions of life so I could see this day that I am so glad to see.

I am so glad to be giving Jesus all the praise and glory that He truly deserves all of my days in the land of the living.

It's a miracle that I have come this far in my life after all the lies I used to believe.

I was going through the motions of life not knowing Jesus, who showed so much mercy to me.

I will love and obey Jesus who carries me through the motions.

Jesus never leaves me alone.

You Will Protect Me

My Lord Jesus, You will protect me from burdens that I can surely bring upon myself.

I see and can't protect myself from the burdens that can weigh me down with stress and worry.

You, my Lord Jesus, are a merciful Lord and Savior who I can come to at any time of day and night with my burdens.

You can lift them away and take them off of me.

I truly thank You, Lord for setting me free of the burdens that can cut me up like a sword and feed me to the hungry lions of depression.

You, my Lord Jesus Christ, will protect me from this as I go through uncertain circumstances in my life.

I thank you, Lord Jesus, for not giving up on me and not passing me by.

You protect me from self-inflicted burdens when I don't know why.

Jesus Will Not Forget

You and I can forget to do something.

Jesus Christ will not forget to bless us and renew our lives if we don't forget to repent of our sins.

You and I can forget to say something to be heard by someone who needs to hear what we have to say.

Jesus won't forget to say what will be according to His holy word.

We can forget to remember, but the Holy Ghost will bring it to our minds from January to December.

You and I can forget something but Jesus will never forget to forgive us of our sins and cast our sins in the still waters that run deep.

Jesus will forget our sins if we confess and repent.

Jesus will remember to be our friend.

Moving Too Fast

Moving too fast can us get into some trouble.

Moving too fast can surely double our burdens.

Moving too fast can cause us to surely regret it.

That regret will surely last a long time .

Moving too fast is nothing good and worthwhile to you and me.

We don't move fast enough when it comes to trusting Jesus, who sees all of our sins.

He will forgive us, fast and for real, if we confess and repent.

Moving too fast can get us into a big mess that Jesus Christ won't get us out of too fast.

He wants to teach us to be patient from our head to our feet.

It's Easy to Feel Like

As long as things are going good in our lives, it's easy to feel like we don't need Jesus Christ, Our Lord and Savior who makes things good in our lives.

As long as we know that our health is good, it's easy to feel like Jesus has nothing to do with it.

As long as we are safe, it's easy to feel like we don't need Jesus' protection day after day.

Jesus is our best security in every way.

It's easy to feel like we are saved and bound for heaven when we may not fully trust and obey Jesus twenty-four hours around the clock.

Jesus Will

The sunlight will glitter on the ocean waves.

The wind will move the gentle waters and make them flow day after day.

The air will be invisible as we breathe it in and out of our nostrils for you and me to live day after day.

The grass will cover the ground with so much class, when Jesus will be the first and not the last to be a friend to you and me.

We will make mistakes that we don't even see that could determine our fate.

Jesus can prolong our lives to a later date.

The sky will stay open all day and all night long with the promises of Jesus, who will come back again one day soon up in the sky.

Having Peace with the Lord

Having peace with the Lord in this troubled world is a great thing to have outside the gates of pearls.

Having peace with the Lord is like heaven on earth every day and every night in this fallen world.

Living right by the Lord will give you and me peace of mind and ease our burdens that will wear us down all the time if we have no peace with the Lord.

He shines His peace in our hearts if we love and obey Him with our whole hearts.

Peace is from the Lord every day

Having peace with the Lord is the way to love in this world where it's so easy to go astray in some kind of way from the Lord, whose peace is forever and evermore.

We Can't Make Any Excuse

We can't make any excuse to be above God's word that you and I cannot get enough of.

If we love Jesus Christ, our Lord, we can't make any excuse to get around God's word.

His word is the way for us to know that His truth will set us free from living in sin.

We can't make any excuse to God, who can reason with us in His word.

We can't fight with God and win.

We can't make any excuse for doing our own will against God's word that is very real.

God's will is beyond any excuse that we can come up with.

We can't make any excuse to sin.

There is no good reasons to sin against God, our friend.

It's What We Put In

It's what we put in our minds that will speak upon our tongues for maybe a day, a week, a month or a year or more.

What we put in our hearts will show in our actions so thick and not thin.

If we put Jesus in our minds, we will speak Jesus upon our tongues so divine.

If we put Jesus in our hearts, Jesus will be in our actions here and there and afar.

Wherever we go we have to put Jesus in our lives.

We have to live by His holy word that we can trust to put our minds and hearts at ease.

We must believe in Jesus Christ, who puts us in His salvation through the price he paid to save us from our sins and put us in heaven in the end.

God is in Control

This world still exists because God is in control, up and down the dangerous roads that get potholes.

God will not let evil men destroy this world that God will destroy in the end.

The world will end in God's time because God is in control.

He knows motives in our hearts.

We can't fool God day after day.

Life still exists because God is in control in every way.

Wars, diseases and natural disasters can't break God's will.

He will not fall from His holy throne beyond the Milky Way.

Sin and death and the grave can't rise up above God, who is in control of life and love.

God is everlasting life and everlasting love.

He gave us this in His only begotten son, Jesus Christ and the Holy Ghost.

God always in control.

The Lord's Ways

The Lord's ways are holy each and every day.

Our ways can be bad, no matter what good that we say day by day.

The Lord's ways are righteous beyond our ways that can be so wrong under the sun.

The Lord's ways are perfect when our ways can be so flawed with sin that can cause our ways to be so unpredictable day after day.

The Lord's ways are what the Bible says.

Our ways can be so false compared to the Lord ways, which are so true before and after we lay down to sleep for the day.

The Lord will wake us up in the goodness of His ways that will never go out of date.

The Lord's ways can be mysterious but help us to wise up before it's too late.

I Will Be Surprised

I will be surprised if I make it to heaven.

There come a time that it will be too late to be saved in Jesus Christ, who I want to love and obey.

Even so, I will be surprised if I make it to heaven one day.

My sinful ways cause me to not always trust Jesus like I need to.

Jesus wont' be surprised to see me in heaven.

If I make it there, I will be surprised to see all who have been set free and are not going to hell.

Many people will be surprised to be there, but Jesus won't be surprised to see them.

Jesus sees all who are going to heaven or hell before we die.

We Can't Run and Hide

We can't run and hide from how we feel.

We must face up to those feelings so very real.

Day by day we can't run and hide from our problems that will stare us down.

Our eyes will see that we need the Lord, who we can't run and hide from all through the day and all through the night.

The Lord sees all who are living in his light of the truth.

We can't run and hide from that.

We must face up to the truth to set us free in our hearts.

We can't run and hide from this no matter what we say and do.

God sees our hearts so crystal clear wherever we go, to and fro.

If Things are Comfortable All the Time

If things are comfortable all the time in our lives, then we need to truly check our spiritual life that should shine in the darkest hour.

If things are not comfortable on our spiritual journey, that's okay. We will have a lot of uncomfortable situations and disappointments to let us know that we are living for our Lord.

He wasn't always comfortable around people who tried to wrong him.

If things are comfortable all the time for us, then we are not going through any trials that call us to suffer for Jesus' name.

That suffering will get us out of our comfort zones.

We can't put our trust in being comfortable all the time.

Sin can make us feel so comfortable that we'll be lost in the end.

Don't Worship the Church

Don't worship the church. It has people with flaws of sin that break God's ten Commandment laws.

The church is supposed to keep the commandments before the whole world to let it know there is a Lord God.

His only begotten son is the head of the church and we worship Jesus Christ who's not dead but is forever alive.

We should not worship with our works that cannot save our souls from being lost.

Only Jesus can save us if we make Him our choice over the church.

The church gets its power from Jesus, who we should worship every minute, second and hour of the day.

If we worship the church, our fruit would be so sour.

Spiritual Support

It's good to give emotional support to people who need it to make their emotions strong through the day.

It's much better to give people spiritual support so they can truly live a life of obedience unto the Lord.

The Lord can always support our emotional and spiritual needs when we pray and ask Him to by faith and trust each and every day.

You and I believe in Jesus Christ and should live our lives supporting His gospel.

Jesus Christ will give eternal life to all who are saved in Him who got emotional support and spiritual support from His heavenly Father.

God bought us with a price through His only begotten son, Jesus, who fought Lucifer and his angels up in heaven and won with His angels' support.

Freedom

It's a blessing to have the freedom to see the squirrels in the park, and have the freedom to take care of dogs that love to bark.

It's a blessing to have the freedom to come and go as we please.

These real freedoms that we know to treasure every day are what Jesus gives us.

He gives us these real true freedoms if we keep His ten golden rules.

Many people believe these rules are a burden and want to do away with God's holy law that is freedom to our souls.

Many people will take freedom for granted and live in their sins, breaking the laws of the land and getting locked up in jail.

They live in bondage.

It's a blessing to have freedom that is fair to everyone. Many people abuse the freedom that Jesus Christ gives to all sinners to be saved in Him who forever lives out freedom in all who will do God's holy will.

Prayer Time

Prayer time is not only when we are at church where we go to and worship the Lord whose ministry work was also about praying to his heavenly Father God.

Prayer time is every day.

You and I should start praying in the morning to noon and at night.

We need the Lord Jesus to bless our lives that would be so empty every day without prayer time.

We pray Unto the Lord who will answer our prayers so divine, if we love Him and obey Him like we know that we should.

Prayer time is not only about showing up at church.

We can pray at any time and wherever we go.

Words Are Powerful

You can say something good that can change a person's life and make them want to do good.

It's not strange to a Christian to speak words of love that are powerful enough to shove away evil words from the lips of fools.

Words are powerful and can lift you up when you are feeling down and depressed.

The devil loves to bring on words to test our faith in Jesus Christ, who spoke nothing but powerful words to so many folks.

He touched many folks with his words of life and truth that could cut like a knife and heal the sin sick soul to repent and turn away from sin.

Words are powerful today and the word of God is powerful no matter what anyone says.

Is Like Chasing the Wind

Putting our trust in this world is like chasing the wind.

We can never catch it from the beginning to the end.

Loving the creature more than loving our creator God is like chasing the wind.

No man, woman, boy or girl can catch the wind in their hands.

The wind will slip through our fingers and blow all around.

Life is like chasing the wind that only Jesus Christ, our Lord, can catch to save us from our sins.

He saved us through the price that he paid.

The wind rejoices day by day.

Doing one's own will is like chasing the wind.

We will never catch it and fill our lives with contentment.

Only Jesus can do this so real.

A Supernatural Thing

It will be a supernatural thing when Jesus comes back again on the clouds of glory that will fill the sky with his angels.

It will be a supernatural thing for the righteous dead to be raised for all to see among the righteous living who will be changed from mortal to immortality.

That will be a supernatural thing to come to you and me if we are alive among the righteous living to see Jesus' supernatural power and glory filling the earth.

One day soon, Jesus Christ will come back again to give his gift of eternal life to all who are saved in Him.

He paid a supernatural price to save all men from being lost in their sins.

I Can't Cast a Stone

I can't cast a stone at anyone else because I have sins to repent of all by myself.

I repent unto the Lord Jesus Christ, who I don't deserve to call upon because Jesus is forever superb above me.

I can't cast a stone at anyone's sins when I must meet Jesus all alone at His judgment seat on His holy throne.

Jesus sits beside His heavenly Father God, who loves me but hates my sins.

I can't cast a stone at anyone in this world where I am a sinner who needs Jesus to save me from my sins all through my life.

I can't cast a stone at anyone else's sins when I am guilty of my sins below the heavens for God to stone me from my head to my toes.

Can Run Deep

A thought can run deep and not find the answer that the Lord knows all the time.

When a mystery can run deep that the Lord knows so well, like going on a boat ride on the water's flow.

The oceans can run deep for the Lord to see every living creature on the bottom of the ocean that he owns every day and every night.

The Lord Jesus Christ's love can run deep and save every soul from being lost in sin.

Sin can run deep with wickedness and death and take the breath right out of our bodies and send us to the grave.

Can't Save Us from Our Sins

Our good works can't save us from our sins.

Only Jesus can save us from the beginning to the end of our lives.

Our good works can't cleanse us from our sins.

Only Jesus can do that.

We can trust day after day that you and I can't save ourselves, no matter what good things we do on the face of this world.

If we could save ourselves from being lost in sin, then Jesus would have no need to give up His life.

That was a choice that he made on the cross to save us from our sins.

Our good works can't do for us, no matter how much power we have to win souls to the Lord,

The Lord doesn't need you and me when only Jesus is always good to save us and set us free.

Behind

Behind some smiles there are so many tears,

And behind our trials there is Jesus who is always near and dear to sinners like me and you.

Behind some success there are some failures to remember where we come from.

Behind our tribulations there is Jesus, who knows how to get us out of a bind on time for us to move on to a higher ground.

Behind our choices that we make is God's holy ground that is always stable to walk on even right now.

Behind some talk there is some action.

Behind all who are saved there is no fraction of being lost because of Jesus Christ, who's always behind the righteous to give us eternal life.

The Book of All Truth

The Bible is the book of all truth, there for all men to know the root of our existence and where we come from.

It also shows us where we will make our destiny that will stand before God, who is all truth in His son Jesus Christ.

Jesus is the way, the truth and the life that we should live each and every day.

The Bible is the book of all truth to always be reliable for you and me to study and live by.

In this world where there are so many lies being told about where we come from, the Bible is the book of all truth.

None of us is without sin to save ourselves from being lost.

The Bible tells us that Jesus paid our price on the cross to save us from our sins.

The Bible says for us to know the truth today.

It Doesn't Take Much Effort

It's doesn't take much effort to say something wrong each and every day.

It doesn't take much effort to do something wrong because you and I were born in sin to fall short of the glory of God, who forever knows that our hearts are not always filled with the right things to please him.

It doesn't take much effort to think about things that are not right for our minds to sink down in the quicksand of sin.

It doesn't take much effort for Jesus to forgive us of our sins if we truly confess and repent and turn away from living in sin.

It doesn't take much effort to die in our sins under the sunlight rays.

We Will Have Some Problems

We will have some problems in the church where everybody is different with a ministry work to build up the church that Jesus Christ is the head of

We will have some problems not looking like love for one another who must love everyone to be like Jesus, who had some problems with his disciples who couldn't always see eye to eye with Him and one another because of their pride getting in the way.

Jesus set them free from the devil's lies that can get in the church and cause strife among church members and church leaders.

Our lives can only be renewed in Jesus who paid our price for us to give him all of our problems that he can work out so nice.

The Master of Our Destiny

Jesus has made us the master of our destiny.

You and I will choose all alone because Jesus has given us a free will.

We choose our destiny that we are the master of every day.

There will be no appeals made by the Lord. He can't choose our destiny for us.

We will choose our destiny before we bite the dust.

A little child who dies and doesn't know right from wrong is only for Jesus to destine to live in heaven.

The Lord gave us free will choice so we will be the master of our destiny.

Jesus won't take that away from us, and the devil can't either.

Our destiny will be heaven or hell that we will choose.

A Shadow Will Let Us Know

A shadow will let us know that there is something real to see.

The shadow of Jesus is God's will for us to live by day after day.

A shadow can appear no matter where we are.

A shadow will let us know that there is something real wherever we go.

Jesus Christ is real in the life of all who are saved in His name.

A shadow will obey His call more than a lot of real people who are so blessed to be real to move about here and there.

We can see that a shadow is not real but will move when you and I move around and hopefully do what the Lord will have us do.

We Can Always Be Certain About Jesus

We can always be certain about Jesus, who will lighten our burdens if we trust Him so very real.

In this world where we can't always be certain about our dreams being so far away to see coming true, we can always be certain about Jesus.

He will never fail to supply our needs day in and day out.

Jesus will be there for us to put our hope in Him when this world is so uncertain like a soap opera changing its scenes.

We don't know what will happen next, but we can always be so certain about our Lord and Savior Jesus Christ.

He is always certain to give us eternal life if we are saved in Him today, when tomorrow is uncertain no matter what we do and say.

Is Only Promised Through

Tomorrow is only promised through the Lord, who can allow you and me to see tomorrow.

He holds us in his hands, for no one to take.

Tomorrow is only promised through the Lord Jesus Christ, who gives us borrowed time.

Today is a miracle for us to see to be so blessed to still be alive to choose or not choose to know the Lord.

Yesterday, today and tomorrow we will obey and follow Him to the end of this world that will pass away one day.

Tomorrow is only promised through the Lord because we can't keep ourselves alive.

Today is more uncertain than tomorrow.

We don't know what will happen to us today, but we do know Jesus is an eternal promise keeper.

Walk Away

Walk away from the bushes of doubt about the Lord who will never let us be out of his love.

Walk away from unrealistic thoughts not being of the Lord day after day.

You and I can walk away from gossip and backbiting and any talk that's not about the Lord and glorifying His holy name.

We can walk away from living in sin and choose to live for the Lord Jesus Christ, who will save us from our sins in this life if we confess and repent.

We should never walk away from the truth of God.

I Will Trust You, O Lord

I am not going to worry about what I have no control over, because I will trust You, O Lord.

You will go with me and rescue me from the monster of worry.

I can trust You, O Lord, to move out of my way under the sky.

My life is nothing without You, Lord Jesus, who sets me free from the burden of worrying when I trust You.

You will never let me down when I need you.

Every day, something good or bad can come my way, but You will not put on me more than what I can bear.

I will always trust You O Lord.

You will always care about being there for me.

I will trust You, O Lord, who is always fair to me no matter where I go here and there.

Some Things are Best Not Said

Some things are best not said.

We may not be strong enough to take it in what someone may say.

We can empty all of our hearts out to Jesus Christ, who can take in every word that we say to Him.

You and I can always talk to Him and He will fully understand.

He can help us to fully trust Him.

He can give us the strength to get through whatever bad things that come our way, so they don't chew us up and spit us out.

Some things are best not said, except if you're saying them to Jesus who is more than a lot of talk.

Jesus will do what He can to help us overcome our weaknesses.

He can make us strong from day to day.

Something is Wrong with Everyone

Something is wrong with everyone because of being born with a sinful nature under the sun.

There is no one without sin in the flesh — not the elite, brightest or the best.

People can sin against the Lord anywhere and any time of the day and night.

God knows the hairs on our heads and on down to our feet.

Something is wrong with everyone who has sins to confess and repent of unto our Lord Jesus Christ.

Everything is right about Him who had no sin in His life when he lived here on earth and paid the price for all of our sins that are wrong in God's eyesight.

Jesus Can Show Up

Jesus can show up when we give up on something we have no control over.

Just when our cup of hope is empty and we're waiting for something good to happen, Jesus can show up for us and be our friend.

He can help us get through the rainy trials that come our way and last for a while.

Jesus can use these trials to open our eyes to see that he won't put on you and me more than what we can bear.

Jesus can show up when we are full of doubt with our hands being useless and getting nothing good done.

Jesus can show up to save us in his kingdom to come upon our life that can end at any day under the sun.

A Better World to Come

There is a better world to come one day in the new world that Jesus will create to have no sins.

Day in and day out that better world will be filled with righteous people who will surely see that God is a righteous and fair God.

He gives everyone a chance to give their heart to his son, Jesus Christ, who will save as many as He can save before this old world passes away into nonexistence.

Jesus will wipe away sin to give us a better world to come.

Like the Bible says, no man can give us a better world to come, no matter how great that he is under the sun.

That's Just the Way It Is

We will do good or we will do evil, for that's just the way it is.

Every day we live to do what the Bible says or what the world says — we will choose or not choose to obey God's ten golden rules. That's just the way it is.

It will be a win or lose for you and me to be saved or not saved in Jesus Christ, who died to save us from our sins and rose from the grave to give us eternal life if we love and obey him everyday and every night.

That's just the way it is for you and me.

One day we will go to heaven with Jesus to be with God, who gave us his only begotten son or we will choose sin and eternal death.

That's just the way it is for Jesus to save sinners upon the land.

One True Color

A lie has many colors to choose and the truth has only one true color that will never fade.

The truth's one true color will always outlast a lie, which can be told in many different ways.

The truth is always told in only one way, day by day.

A lie has many colors, and will surely fade away in the light of the truth.

The truth will always have a very bright, shining color like the beautiful bright sunlight, which has one true color shining over you and me, no matter where we live around the world.

The truth has one true color to tell and to live by God's true word, which will always be triumphant.

A lie will fail sooner or later, no matter how many ways it has of being told.

The truth has only one true color.

Love is always true from God, who cannot lie.

There is one true color and that is the truth and life of Jesus Christ, in our minds, hearts and souls throughout our lives.

Go With the Flow of Life

All that we can do is take it one day at a time and go with the flow of life.

We have no control over life, and it doesn't worry about you and me making mistakes.

Life that will flow in the sea of God's love.

He knows where life will take us according to our choices.

The Lord God won't interfere with you and me choosing what we want to do in life.

There is a flow of life given to all who will bear their crosses and follow Jesus Christ, who is the life that we will flow on for eternity.

Loving him who paid the price for us to go with the flow of life is the way to go.

God sees beyond our ups and downs in this life on earth that goes with the flow.

It flows all around our souls to save for us for eternal life in Jesus right now.

We can go with the flow of life on God's holy ground.

Forever and Ever

A man may see a beautiful and sweet woman for the first time and may feel like he has loved her forever and ever.

Through the sunshine and rain, his love for her is sweeter than the best dreams, and more mystical than a thousand moons that seem to wander across the light years in the outer space.

Jesus Christ loves you and me forever and ever.

He wants to save us and give us eternal life.

Because God so loved us first forever and ever he gave us his only begotten son, Jesus Christ who has won the victory and has power over death.

We can't run away and hide from God. He is everlasting love beyond the sun.

A man can love a woman forever and ever like the endless stars that never lose their sparkles of light shining so very far above the mystical night.

They hover over our visions and dreams of the greatest love of God coming back on the clouds of glory above.

The highest clouds in the sky will be so happy for you and me to go with Jesus back to heaven and live forever and ever being in love with God.

Who am I?

Who am I, to be like a ship wrecked and sinking?

I should let Jesus steer my life on His course and I shouldn't think twice about it.

Who am I, being like a quick eye blink to an eternal God that allows me to exist and to choose to do His will?

I deserve to die being lost in my sins. They are a big lie that will never set me free.

The truth of God's word can set me free, though.

I don't always know me in my own eyes, and I ask myself, "Who am I?"

Only Jesus Christ always knows how to help me flee from selfish me.

I can only be selfless in my Lord and Savior Jesus Christ, who can save me from my sins that I was born in.

I have to confess, and repent unto Jesus and work out my own soul's salvation that Jesus gave to me.

Who can doubt me, whether I am right or wrong?

It's for me to wonder about who I am.

The Bible will also tell me about me, for me to surely know who I am.

I will never fool God wherever I go.

We Can Shorten Our Own Lives

We can shorten our own lives if we don't take good care of our health that we don't own.

We can make mistake after mistake and shorten our own lives that truly belong to the Lord Jesus Christ each and everyday.

The Lord lives forever and ever beyond our short lifespan that we can give to the grave so easily if we do our own will and not the Lord's will.

We should be keeping His holy law that can add more years to our lives that are flawed with sin.

We can add on to our lifespan if we confess and repent unto the Lord who can set us free from shortening our own lives.

This we can do if we love and obey Him each and everyday that is short under the Milky Way

A Wandering Moment

Our moment in time is a wandering moment.

We do not know how long our time will last.

We can't trust anything more than trusting the Lord.

He knows that we can make choices to wander our moment of our short lives.

We can see that so many young people are dying everyday.

Only the Lord knows our last day to live.

Our moment in time can wander away so fast under the sun that shines over the good and bad and the great and small.

A wandering moment can take us all.

We have a conscience to listen to the Holy Spirit's voice to obey the Lord or disobey the Lord who has a course to take us on beyond our wandering moment.

Jesus can save us from being lost in our wandering moment that we make by our choices.

Only Jesus can count all of our mistakes.

Predestined

Your plans were predestined to work out, O Lord, before You created the world.

Without a doubt Your wisdom was predestined to be infinite throughout the outer space where man can't see all the shining stars.

O Lord, Your almighty, powerful hand was predestined to hold all existence in its place before the hands of human beings could hold anything on the face of this world.

You, O Lord God, were predestined to send Your only begotten son to save the lost and do all men justice.

Before time was created by You, O Lord, You were predestined by Your grace and truth to follow through on Your love for the wise and the fools.

Whether You're Rich or Poor

Whether you're rich or poor, everyone will struggle with something in their lives under the sun.

Many people will let the struggle get the best of them and they will not trust the Lord who we all can rest our mind in.

Whether you're rich or poor, it doesn't matter to the Lord.

He will open or close a door for us who will struggle with something every day.

Whether you're rich or poor, you can lay it down at Jesus' feet or hold onto it in every way that could lead to destruction.

Struggles don't care about coming in our lives to break us or make us.

Whether you're rich or poor, we can trust Jesus to help us overcome our struggles if we let Him set us free.

No Matter

No matter where we live, God's word is for us all to live by, regardless of whether we live in the city or in the country/

God's all-seeing eyes sees everything going on in the north, south, east and west side of this world.

No matter who we are, God's word is for us all to live by deep down in our hearts to show and tell on our life, day after day.

No matter how we look, God's word is for us all to live by in this shattered world of troubled times going on everywhere these last days.

No matter what church we go to under God's grace, God's word is there for us all to live by, before we lay down to go to sleep in the night, for God's word to be in our unconscious minds.

No matter what time we wake up or what time we lay back down, God's word is for us all to live by so divine.

We Can See with Our Eyes

We can see with our eyes, but don't always see with our hearts that can blind you and me with selfishness.

We don't always see within our hearts what Jesus can see.

We can be blind even though we can see with our eyes.

Our hearts can't always see the lies that Jesus always sees

He lets us see the truth that can set us free from our own hearts that can blind us.

We can fail to stand up for Jesus Christ.

We need to be a witness unto Him who sees all things in heaven and earth.

You and I cannot always see our own hearts getting in the way of Jesus when he comes to cleanse us of our sins.

We need to see with our hearts that Jesus is always a friend to us who can see with our eyes and may not see what a blind man can see in the heart.

The Highest Life

The highest life to live is a spiritual life.

That life is most favorable unto the Lord Jesus Christ, who lives the highest life unto his heavenly Father God who is the highest spirit to know our whole hearts.

Every day God wants you and me to especially live the highest life unto Him.

He will always give us His holy will that is spiritual above our will that is all about living a selfish life that loves material things that can shorten our lives.

This is no good thing.

The highest life should be a spiritual life unto the Lord who will one day give us eternal life.

The highest life to live is in Jesus' name that is spiritual in the highest all through this life and the afterlife to come.

There is No Distance in Love

The stars in the universe are so distant and far apart, far away from many distant hearts, and the sky is so distant from the ground.

There is no distance in God's love for all men around the world.

Can we love one another at a distance?

There is no distance in love; it covers a multitude of sins.

Distance means to move away from love. That won't do for you and me.

Love will draw us closer together to stick together in unity.

If Jesus Christ loved us at a distance, He would not have come to this world to crush the serpent's head on the cross, way below the distant heavens.

Love is love and there is no distance in the love of Jesus Christ, who commands us to love one another.

There is no distance in love in heaven above the earth.

Many people will distance themselves from God, who is love with no distance.

Even death cannot come between God and us.

The Thorn in My Flesh

O Lord, I thank you for putting a thorn in my flesh to help me to humble myself before you.

You are my best of the best friend that I will ever have.

The thorn in my flesh is a blessing from You, O Lord, day in and day out.

Pride will surely take me to a fall if I believe that I made myself to conquer all things in this world.

That sets me up for a fall day after day.

I am so blessed to know my call by You, Lord Jesus, who I thank for putting a thorn in my flesh so I can see that I need to be reborn in You.

I need to pick up my cross and follow You even unto death, which can't do me in.

My soul is saved in You, my Lord Jesus, who wore a crown of thorns on Your head for me to know that you felt my pain more than I can ever imagine.

Flip Through the Pages of Life

We will flip through the pages of life if we are not rooted and ground in Jesus Christ.

He wants to keep us on the same page with Him if we do His holy will.

His word is on every page in His holy bible that you and I can study to show ourselves approved.

Flipping through the pages of life will take us to a dead end of disappointments and sorrow.

This is what we will sooner or later get for not denying ourselves so real.

We can flip our blank pages so fast against His will when we want to do our own will.

We can flip through the pages of life, far from the page of repentance that we need to study to come to Jesus with a whole heart of surrender.

This is a page that we should never flip from the start to the end of our lives.

Spiritual Kinfolks

You and I are spiritual kinfolks.

We are children of a God who always keeps his oath.

You and I have been kinfolk by blood.

All of them are not spiritual in our eyes day after day.

All of God's children are spiritual kinfolks and are related to Jesus in our hearts, minds and souls.

We can become new creatures in Jesus, who is one with God all through eternity.

You and I will be spiritual kinfolks by being saved and washed clean in the blood of Jesus Christ our Lord, whose blood is the only blood that will make us all kin in our newness of life that all of our blood kin are not living in.

Who We Hang Out With

We are who we hang out with.

This shows and tells who we are here and there and everywhere we go.

If we hang out with stupid people, we will be stupid, and if we hang out with mean people, we will be mean sooner or later for people to see.

If we hang out with intelligent people, we will be intelligent, and if we hang out with real people we will be real genuine to people in this world.

Many people don't love to hang out with Jesus who is love all the time.

We can hang out with Jesus Christ in the Bible on our good and bad days.

If we hang out with sin, we are living in sin against God who created us to hang out with his Son.

Jesus will hang out with us if we trust and obey him every day and every night.

We are who we hang out with near and far.

Keeping God's Commandments is hanging out with the brightest morning star, and the lily of the valley arraying the glow of God over sinners, who can choose to hang out with a heart of repentance unto the Lord and do his will.

Know There is a God

Changes know there is a God, who will never change.

Luck knows there is a God, whose miracles are so supernatural, and penetrate through our hearts.

A phenomenon knows there is a God, who is extraordinary beyond our senses that can blow a fuse of nonsense.

The unknown knows there is a God to make known what He wants us to know and what we need to know for our own good and wellbeing.

This will never disagree with God.

From moment to moment we knows there is a God, whose Son bore our sins on the cross.

Because God cares to save our souls in our moment in time, He will judge us fairly.

Mysteries know there is a God, whose ways can be more mysterious than any unsolved mystery and deeper than the floors of the profound oceans.

The atheist will believe there is no God, even when the mercy and grace of God shows and tell on his and her life.

God spares us from death when we believe.

The atheist calls it luck, but death will laugh at the atheists. They have no power over their evolution theories, and are drowning in the tidal waves of God's holy word.

Surely this lets us know there is a God, who gave us his Son to save us.

Being Full

The day is full of the light and the night is full of the dark.

God is full of love that will never change from day to night.

Our eyes are full of the visible things we see, below the sky where our mouth is full of words coming from our minds.

Our heads are full of thoughts, and our hearts are full of motives all the time in this world that's full of sin.

Jesus Christ was without sin for being full of the Holy Spirit, who is full of truth without a doubt.

We need to fill our lives up with living right unto the Lord Jesus, who is full of the way, truth and life, for us to be saved all through this life, that is full of trouble for you and me.

Being full of doing God's will, which the Bible is full of, gives us more and more of Jesus in our minds and hearts.

Jesus is full of grace and salvation.

The devil is full of being lost, day after day and night after night, which is full of the sun, moon and stars below the highest heaven,

Being full of Jesus coming back one day soon with all the angels to take us to heaven,

Being full of eternal life in God.

How Did God Begin?

How did God begin?

God existed before the universe that is so immeasurable and infinite, beyond all existence here on earth.

No one knows how God begins.

The Bible and nature can't prove how God began.

Lucifer wanted to be God, but when Lucifer failed to complete his task, that has surely enslaved him to meet his fate in hell that God also created for the fallen angels who didn't exist before God.

Can a child exist before its parents?

It's more than impossible for children to give birth to their parents.

This shows that God is the beginning of all existence that God created below His existence.

A man can believe that he is God until death looks at him in his face.

There is no death in God, who is the breath of life and eternal life.

How did God begin?

We will die before we will ever know.

We don't need to know.

Our eyes are visual in sin, and don't always see a lie.

God can't lie to always be the everlasting truth.

Many people will not believe how human beings begin and what the Bible tells us about Adam and Eve being created by God.

God doesn't force anyone to believe in his Son and obey the voice of his Holy Spirit who is a trinity of one with God.

Only God knows how He began in the eternal beyond.

A Language that Everyone Can Speak

A smile is a language that everyone can speak in the home, on the job and in the streets.

Shedding a tear is a language that everyone can speak down in the lowest valley to the highest mountain peak.

Feeling good and feeling bad is a language that everyone can speak in the heat of the day and in the cold of the night that feelings can run deep.

Having good motives and bad motives is a language that everyone can speak under the sun, where every language can speak to God, who's up in heaven above.

God can reach down to us with his language of love to all the world.

Every man, woman, boy and girl can speak to God in their own language, thanks to Jesus Christ who can relate to all men to be saved in Him, who paid our price.

He speaks salvation to all the world in God's language of eternal life.

So Quiet

Nature is so quiet, when bills are so noisy, to echo their voices all through the house with no remorse.

The roads are so quiet, when heavy traffic can be noisy and may cause tension to rise among many drivers who are having a bad day.

The air that we breathe is so quiet, when strong winds can blow so noisy and knock down some houses so loud.

So quiet is the sky, when jets will fly so noisy through the sky.

The rain will fall so quiet down on me and you.

Motives are so quiet, when words can be so noisy and cause stress that can be so quiet from the north, south, east and west side of this world, when riots, wars and protests can be so noisy.

Sleep is so quiet, when snoring can be so noisy all night long.

The night is so quiet, when people are having a ball in the noisy nightclubs and bars filled with loud music.

We can sometimes move around so noisily, when all the clouds will move across the sky so quiet.

A bullet can hit anyone so quietly, when gunshots are so noisy.

The Lord Jesus Christ will blot out our sins and write our names in the book of life so quiet.

All hell will be so noisy with lost souls, burning up with all of their sins.

God is the Smartest One

God is the smartest one to solve every problem that we have no matter where we live in this world.

Many crooks and criminals are smart at doing bad things day after day.

God is the smartest one who knows everyone's hearts.

The smartest people on earth will never fully know every motive and intent.

Many people will go here and there and all around the world searching for more knowledge to make them smarter, that can be foolishness.

The Lord God's son, Jesus Christ, showed the world that God is the smartest one in heaven.

He knows that this spiritually ill world needs a Savior to save us sinners from our sins.

All the wisdom and knowledge of this world can't do that in the fall, winter, spring and summertime.

God is the smartest one, His Son never did doubt during his darkest hour under the sun.

No One Can Rehearse Life

We can rehearse a song to sing and make it to sound so good to bring joy to a broken heart that will not rehearse that least bit to get broken and feel like being thrown in a deep pit.

We can rehearse a script to make a great movie, to move hearts in the right way to learn something good, before it's too late.

No one can rehearse life to never make any mistakes.

We all make mistakes in life that we don't have to rehearse from our birth to our last day to live on earth.

No one can rehearse what a day will bring.

We can rehearse a song to sing unto the Lord Jesus Christ, who created life to be no rehearsal.

You and I can live and do God's will without a rehearsal by believing in Jesus Christ

It's in our nature to sin, we don't have to rehearse that in this sinful world.

If God

Who can be right if God is wrong?

God can't be wrong all day and all night long.

Who can love, if God is full of hate?

God is love that the devil hates to see shining down on us from heaven above the earth.

Who can live, if God is dead?

His Son rose from the grave and went back to heaven beyond this world, which is filled with sinners, who can choose to be saved in God's Son, Jesus Christ. He will set us free.

Who can be free, if God is in bondage?

The devil would put God in bondage, if God let Him do so.

God will never do this because God is God who can do all things perfectly and is always great.

You and I can't do even the simple things, if God can't do anything for us.

We can do nothing but fail all the time, if God fails.

For the Bible to be a fairy tale story about God and not be true, then who can be true?

God is true and real.

The devil knows that God is real and true and put him in a hot furnace fire.

Who can be saved if God created time to be too late?

We All

We all are in the same boat drifting on the ocean water of life.

This life can give us motion sickness, disappointments and sorrows.

We all are in the same boat like Jesus' disciples were to the storm, that knew Jesus' name to be all powerful and above the heavens on high.

We all are in the same boat of needing Jesus below the sky.

We can't afford to drift away from Jesus Christ, Our Lord, who can calm the storms into our lives.

Jesus will sometimes allow us to get motion sickness from our trials.

He encourages us to love and trust him more and more.

We all are in the same boat to not be opinionated about one another's motives.

Our own ways will float on the deep waters of selfishness, if we don't trust Jesus to steer our boat through the sharks of temptation that can attack us.

We all are in the same boat and must step off the boat like Peter did, to walk on the water that kept its peace and trust in Jesus.

Peter took his eyes off of Jesus and began to sink.

If Jesus allows a storm to sink our boat, it will serve His holy purpose.

We Need the Lord's Vaccine

We need to get injected with the Lord's vaccine of spiritual things that will make our spiritual immune systems strong against things that are temporary.

Those temporary things make our spiritual immune systems weak so they can't fight off the devil's bacteria temptations that will infect us with sin.

This will make us spiritually dead.

We need the Lord's vaccine to make us spiritually well so we can do good deeds with good pure motives. The Lord loves to inject our hearts with his vaccine of spirit and truth so that the bacteria of sin will be rejected.

You and I can choose to repent of our sins and let Jesus Christ inject our souls to be saved so we can live a renewed life in Jesus.

We need the Lord's vaccine of redemption to redeem us back to God.

The Greatest Social Person

Jesus Christ was the greatest social person who ever lived on earth.

This is because Jesus knew what to say and what not to say to everyone who he so first loved.

Jesus socialized with the publicans and sinners who he sat down and ate food with.

The scribes and Pharisees didn't want to be hanging around them because they believed that they were too high up in status to socialize with people they believed to be low-life types and were not up on educational level or spiritual level.

Today in this fallen world's society there are also many church folks who believe themselves to be better than those who are less educated than them.

Jesus shows no respect of persons to socialize and have a relationship with Him so pure with the right motives every day.

Jesus loves to talk to and spend time with anyone who loves Him so dear, whether they're rich or poor. The sun shines down on everyone and sheds its light upon all the living from sun up to sun down.

Man Cannot Live by Man Alone

Man cannot live by man alone.

Man needs God and to live by God's golden rules.

God put them in man's heart because man cannot live by man alone.

Man will destroy man and wipe him off the face of the earth if God leaves man all alone upon the land.

Man cannot be God, who needs no man to tell Him what to say and do because God is God alone so very, very well.

God has no need to live by man, who can get a swelled head from doing something great in the eyes of men, but in the eyes of God that great thing may be something small to bend and break.

Man can live through God's Son, Jesus Christ, who is the bread of life for man to live by from the beginning to the end of man's life.

Man cannot live by man alone. If he does, he will surely fail like the fallen angels falling from heaven on high.

Discover

Man will discover what God allows him to discover.

Nothing is new to God, who created the known and unknown, to fill our minds with wonder.

Man will not discover what God won't allow him to discover, because God is always in charge of the seen and unseen here on earth, and throughout all existence in every universe God called into existence through his eternal omnipotent voice.

Man can always discover God, calling Him to repent, and believe in Jesus Christ, who is the word of God for all men to discover.

The holy Bible scriptures point out our sins to us, who will only discover what God allows us to discover, and share with one another.

We can always trust God, who can sometimes work in mysterious ways that we can't discover if God doesn't allow us to know His way.

He can set a soul free from being lost.

God knows all things beyond you and me.

On the Edge

If you are on the edge of hope, Jesus is standing on the edge to catch you and help you cope.

In life things may seem to be over the edge of living, but Jesus is standing on the edge to catch you to keep on living your life.

You can be a blessing to others who may be on the edge of giving up on doing what is right.

Jesus always sees over the edge of living in darkness, where there is no light shining over the edge of sinning against God, who's always right in his holy word.

Grace is on the edge of this world, but Jesus Christ overcame because of God's love.

God is standing on the edge to catch the sinner to be saved in his Son, who is our only living hope.

We are standing on the edge of our salvation from our birth to our last day as we live on the edge of our moment in time.

Before We

Before we see anything, the Lord has already seen everything so crystal clear.

We may only catch a glimpse of what He sees.

Before we hear anything, the Lord has already heard every voice that can never talk too fast for the Lord to hear and understand every word, whether it be good or bad.

Before we do anything, the Lord has already done every good thing. It would be too much for us to handle if the Lord showed us all the good that He did.

Before we make a choice, the Lord has already chosen you and me to be born into this world, whether we live a short life or a long one to serve His purpose.

We are here to love and obey our Lord Jesus Christ, who was before all things.

Before we could talk and walk and before we die, the Lord already knows our destiny — whether we will live for Him or fall into a deep dark hole to be lost while eternity passes by.

Free as the Wind

Free as the wind that blows from the north to the south are repentant souls whose hearts have been set free, beyond words from the mouth.

As free as the wind blowing from the east to the west are all who love and obey Jesus Christ with all of their hearts to be as free as the wind blowing under all the stars.

Free as the wind that blows across the wide-open sky and free as the wind blowing across the dry land are you and I.

Being saved in Jesus Christ, who is the living truth of His word, sets us free from the devil's lies.

We must do God's will, that blows so free like a kind wind soothing our minds, to be at peace and rest in the love of God, who's always on time.

He blows us free from worries and fear in the strong winds of his protection that can outlast long light years in the universe.

We can be as free as the wind that blows a little feather away like it's never been seen.

God knows all and sees all existence blowing like that little feather so free in the wide-open sky.

God's love is blowing His kind winds of mercy and grace on our souls to be saved in Jesus Christ, who bore our sins.

Will Move

The wind will move the clouds, so peacefully across the sky that hovers over you and me.

The gentle breeze blows by us so free under the great blue sky, where the wind will move the waters to flow.

God's love will move many hearts as the wind blows on the beautiful face of the water's surface that will stand still for you and me to embrace so dear.

The wind will move the tree limbs to flap for joy to see the mighty rushing winds of the Holy Ghost surely moving the gospel of Jesus Christ from sea to sea and coast to coast.

No one will be left out of accepting Jesus Christ to be their Lord and Savior.

One's heart needs to be right with God before it's too late.

Today all who are still alive can choose to move their hearts to repent so real.

There was a time that God repented that He made man whose ways are like the wind, blowing in different directions across the land.

The Human Body

Don't worship the human body. It can age and get old.

The Lord lives forever, beyond this life, like a tale that's told day by day.

The human body is not worthy to be worshipped, no matter how beautiful that body may look.

It could die young and go to an early grave below the heavens above

Jesus Christ is worthy to be worshipped by the angels throughout eternal life that Jesus will one day give to the human body for worshipping Him.

He is Lord over the human body every day.

Our bodies belong to Jesus and are His holy temple to dwell in, to be so right and never wrong.

He blessed the human body that God created to worship and glorify Him.

Jesus is one with God, beyond the human body that will one day soon be gone forever and ever to heaven or hell.

The Lord created heaven and hell to serve His purpose.

Only Jesus is worthy to be worshipped, like the Bible tells us.

The purpose of the human body is to live, to do God's will until there is no more life in that body.

That body will live again in Jesus Christ, who took on a human body form to relate to you and me.

He feels our infirmities, yet He is without sin in His flesh.

He set you and me free from the sins that the human body was born into.

The Unseen

The unseen is like the wind that we can't see.

The unseen sees us no matter where we are at in the day and night.

Good and evil angels are unseen all around you and me who are visible to see below the stars every day and every night.

Our eyes can't see the unseen.

We will not be strong enough to see the unseen if Jesus the King of Glory reveals the unseen to our eyes to see what we can't handle because of our sinful nature.

Without Jesus in our lives, we are like an unseen tree covered over with fog.

Our eyes can never see the unseen Jesus Christ with our eyes, but with faith we can see.

We can choose to love and obey Jesus, whose unseen almighty hand can hold the seen and the unseen with a holy tight, strong grip.

The unseen is like a deep unsolved mystery that will not dip it's invisibility into the business of our free will choices from the Lord, who we've never seen but can always believe in.

Jesus is more and more beyond the seen and is surrounded by the everlasting unseen God.

We are Not Ancient

Many young people will look at old age as something ancient.

We who are fifty-plus are not ancient; you and I are just much wiser.

We are the aged conquerors in the Lord, who has given us the victory to win over immaturity and inexperience in life.

Foolishness is ancient to us who have grown gracefully with God's grace shining upon our faces.

Our hearts are still young with spiritual maturity and strength in the Lord.

Our righteous living has no ancient life upon our age before any age group of people who love the Lord every day that goes by.

The great number of our years proves that God's mercy didn't deny us to live to see this day that we are not ancient.

In God's church of today, we have a merger with the youth.

We look in the mirror we will see years of ups and downs on our faces that the winds of God's love blows on us so gently.

Ancient is something that's long gone.

Our experiences are present today for us to help the youth get beyond their obstacles in life to do God's will, which doesn't age under and above the sun.

There is a Place that We've Never Seen

There is a place that we've never seen over the full white moonlight shining its mysterious light all around us in the night.

That place is where eyes never saw over the horizon of the sunlight beams that we can see looking so radiant.

That's how we look to Jesus, who we can lean on.

Oh what a perfect place that all the saved will one day go to over the deepest ocean floors and over the water surface waves.

Jesus Christ, our Lord, walked on through the storm that laid down its burden unto Jesus.

This place is reserved for a number that no man can count and all the saints will one day go there beyond the rainbows that will one day pass away.

That perfect place will have gates of pearls for you and me to walk through because we held onto Jesus through our sufferings and pain.

There is a place where everyone will not go to for you and me to be surprised if we make it there and see one another being in that place called heaven.

Today is the time to choose to follow Jesus Christ through the fire of our trials that we all will have in this life.

If we are born again in Jesus, He has a heaven to put us in paid for by the price he paid to save us from our sins.

The Eyes of love

The eyes of love see no color of the skin that love covers with a multitude of sins.

We cannot deceive the eyes of love, always looking down on us all from the heaven above where God is everlasting love to always see.

It saves you and me and sets us free from our own eyes that see more heartaches, sorrows and deaths than love.

Selfishness hates to see love when the eyes of love see peace, justice, equality, freedom and kindness to never cease in God, who sees to save the lost and sees to forgive us of our sins in His all-seeing eyes of love, that will always see all who believe in his Son, Jesus Christ, who we can see in the holy Bible and see in the life of anyone living a renewed life in the love of God.

No Matter the Color of the Skin

No matter the color of the skin it's good to see people treating one another right.

It's a good thing in this world where no matter the color of the skin it's good to see people having love for one another.

When it comes to helping people to do better in life, the color of the skin should not matter to you and me.

We have our skin color according to God's will.

It's for us to love the color that He gives to us so real.

No matter the color of the skin it's always good to see people loving the Lord Jesus Christ, regardless of their neighborhood.

Jesus loves to accept us on earth and up in heaven.

When He comes back again, every color of the skin of people will go to live with Him in the eternal life that Jesus will give to every Christian.

He will see no skin color on his holy hill.

Was the Only Thing

If a sermon was the only thing that could help us to grow stronger in the Lord, then we wouldn't need a gospel song that can be so inspiring.

If a Bible lesson was the only thing to let us know that God is real, then we wouldn't need nature that shows us that God is real in this world.

If grace and the law were the only things to save us, then Jesus would not have had to shed his blood for all to cleanse our sins.

Grace and the law can't do for us flawed creatures who are misfit sinners.

If calling on Jesus' holy name was the only thing to give us strength, then we wouldn't have a need to go to church and assemble ourselves in the Lord to get more of the power of the Holy Ghost never being void of giving us spiritual strength.

Spiritual strength is a thing that we need to hold onto Jesus and achieve spiritual success through doing good deeds.

So Caught Up

We can be so caught up in the amazement of how the Lord is blessing us so well, but if we don't share our blessings with others the door of winning a lost soul may close on us.

We can be so caught up in the spirit of the Lord on the holy Sabbath day of rest, that when the Sabbath is over we may go back to the old drawing board of giving the Lord less and less of our time and giving more of more of our time to temporary things that will one day pass away.

We can get so caught up in the activities of the day that can go so good and well for us that we don't humble ourselves and pray to our Lord Jesus Christ, who the holy angels are always caught up in.

We can be so caught up in going to church, and not always exhorting the Lord in our trials and temptations. That will cause us to get caught up in sin if we don't trust the Lord to bring us safely through our trials and temptations.

We can be caught up in knowing the truth and may be in bondage making the wrong choices, because we don't believe that the truth can set us free.

We can get so caught up in the motion of worshipping the Lord Jesus Christ, but our feelings may be ill to not be nice to those who we can't always fool.

There is no dull moment in being caught up in Jesus, when boredom can get caught up in the brain in our skull.

Can Change Our Life Forever

We can experience a bad thing that can change our lives forever.

No disappointments, misfortunes or grief can ever cause the Lord to change on you and me whether we are great or small in this world.

Bad experiences can change our lives forever for the better or worse.

We don't understand why bad things can happen to good people.

Only God's reason alone can give us the answer that can change our lives forever.

We have to own up to our sins and repent unto the Lord, who can change our lives forever.

We have to do his will.

If we look at the cross to see the price that Jesus paid for us to be saved, then we should want to change to love and obey Him forever.

As we live our lives, we need to hold onto Jesus all through our good and bad experiences that can change our lives forever. In Him, we can be renewed.

A Spiritual Uplifting

Going to church can surely give you and me a spiritual uplifting to set us free from our burdens that can wear us down spiritually.

Going to church on God's holy ground can surely give us a spiritual uplifting in Jesus Christ, who is the Lord of the spiritual realm every day and every night.

Around the clock Jesus can lift us up inside and outside the church walls

Our spirits can abide in the Lord's will when our will can crush our spirits for doing our own thing.

We must not do that because we will not get a spiritual uplifting in the Lord if we are living in sin.

Jesus can give us a spiritual uplifting with the victory to win if we love and obey Him, our highest spiritual guide and best friend.

A Big Difference

It's a big difference in telling people what they need to do and helping people to do what they need to do. When you and I help people, it will have a lot better effect on them than just telling them what to do.

People can tell the difference between words and actions.

Only the Lord will always follow through.

The Lord always does what He says in his holy word, while you and I will fall short of doing all that we say to do on any day.

We might not do what we say to follow through on our word.

Only Jesus Christ will forever follow through because He is the Lord of Lords and King of Kings over you and me.

We should be able to tell the difference between saying something and doing something before our fellow man upon the land.

There is a big difference between lip service and hand service.

Only Jesus will always do both so grand.

The Lord Has Brought Us Through

The Lord has brought us through the valley of life's disappointments that were bad to us.

We know that it's right to trust and obey Jesus Christ.

The Lord walked with us through dark tunnels when we didn't see any light in the void to our spiritual sight.

The Lord has brought us through the years that were like a shadow in the night that the Lord disappeared for us to see this day being so real.

All of our good choices are no reason for us to have come this far, when the Lord has brought us through bad seasons of harm and danger that we had no control over to save our own lives, that Jesus Christ, our Lord spared.

We have seen dreams failing us to let us know that they were not for us.

The Lord has brought us through failed dreams to let us know that they were not for us.

Memories will tell on many of us telling stories to sparkle like the stars.

Jesus has brought us through many life experiences that we can keep in our hearts to share with one another.

The Lord has brought us through the deep oceans of many uncertain days that he used to lead us to a heart of devotion time with him today.

We all know that a mountain is very high up in the sky, and today we are mountain people in the Lord, who brought us through the deep valley of lies to set us up high in the truth of His holy word.

He did this for us to know and live by, even at this banquet.

We have crossed over the roads of our yesterdays because of the Lord building more roads for us to walk down so we can one day see Him face to face.

Nature is a Church

Nature is a church that we can go to and worship God.

The trees, flowers and grass will always dress in modest apparel for us to see nature respecting God in its natural beauty being so free of pretense.

Nature is always so real about showing you and me that God is real.

You and I are not always real about giving God all the glory and praise in the church.

We have a sinful nature going against nature's ministry work of always being about glorifying God regardless of natural disasters being so different from spiritual disasters in the church.

So many church folks are exalting self to be like God, who has a church in nature to worship him in the firmament of the stars, moon and sun to never part from God's nature church of redeemed hearts.

A Cool Shade

Jesus is a cool shade in life's hot heat of disappointments and grief.

Jesus can cool us off with his goodness.

Life's heat can beat down on us in this sinful world.

We can find a cool shade under a big tree on a hot day.

Every day Jesus is a cool shade to cool off life's pain and troubles.

The cool shades in this world can't do that for us.

We can cover over our own heat of the wrong desires and doing our own will under the hot sun.

Jesus is a cool shade in our life.

Jesus can prolong and cool off life's hot heat if we put our hearts to doing his will that can keep our lives cool on his holy ground.

Storms in the Heart

We can cause our own storms in our hearts that can be stormy with thunder and lightning of selfishness.

On a clear, sunny, bright day there is no storm up in the sky.

Our hearts can be pouring down in the rain of lies to wet us up with not being trusted.

We can trust the day to be present on a stormy day.

Many of us don't like to see that, especially if we need to leave the house to take care of business.

Without a doubt, our motives can be like a raging storm to the Lord, who knows our whole hearts that he will never ignore.

We can pray to the Lord to calm the storms in our hearts that can appear in tornado words and actions to rip apart families and friends, and most of all push away God.

No Matter How Many Times

No matter how many times we climb up a ladder, one fall can make all the climbs look so vain to us all.

No matter how many times we win, one loss can change our winning streak and set us on a new course.

No matter how many times we lose, one win is a great thing to be accepted to the rules.

No matter how many times you and I sin against the Lord, he will always set us free if we repent and turn away from living in sin.

We can't count all the times that we sinned against the Lord, who wants to save us from our sins no matter how many times you and I willfully sin and break his holy law.

We point our finger at someone's flaws to make ourselves look void of sin, but that won't work with the Lord no matter how many times we point our finger.

There is Nothing Right About

There is nothing right about not believing in Jesus Christ.

Even the demons believe Him to be the son of God.

We will have eternal life for believing in Jesus Christ.

There is nothing right about putting your trust in self.

We are not perfect or without sin.

With or without being saved, we return to the dust of the earth that God made us from.

There is nothing right about not keeping God's holy law.

Only a fool would doubt to not prolong his life in the land of the living.

There is nothing right about living in sin that can surely shorten our lives.

Jesus gave up his life to save you and me from our sins.

There is nothing right about not being a friend to Jesus, who is our very best friend each and every day.

There is nothing right about being a friend to this world that will betray us and leave us to die being lost in our sins.

There is nothing right about putting anyone or anything above God, who is always right about his only begotten son, Jesus Christ.

He will represent our court case up in heaven.

Only Jesus will see God's holy and infinite face.

There is nothing right about turning your back on Jesus, who will always save you from your sins if you confess and repent and turn away from living in sin.

Can Explore

Man can explore the outer space and find many galaxies and black holes that have been there since before time on earth.

Jesus created it all for man to explore.

Many men don't believe that the Lord created it all.

Man can explore the deepest ocean floor and find new creatures that can open new doors to science and medicine.

Jesus created it all for man to explore the bottom of the oceans where His holy law also abides.

Man just can't seem to explore the depth of the heart filled with motives and intentions that can start up wars and bloodshed.

Jesus created the heart to choose right from wrong for as long as we live to not find the highest height

And deepest depth of life that man can explore and find in Jesus, who was a man without sin.

Man can explore sin and surely find death in the end of his exploration.

Man can explore Jesus in the holy Bible and find Jesus being the good news to all the world that is on a spiritual decline.

We are All Free

We are all free to go to a clear conscience of doing what is right and to always be above what is wrong.

We are free to go to our secret place of prayer unto the Lord, who will waste no time to answer our prayers in his time.

We are free to go to our motives to find out that our hearts will not always reason things out to be right with God.

We all are free to be about Jesus Christ or the devil, but only a fool can doubt the freedom that God gave to all of us.

We all are free to go to doing good or evil.

We can trust the good that God is all the time over evil.

We are all free to live when the wages of sin is death to the great and small.

Jesus wants to save us to be free one day go to heaven where freedom is eternal beyond the Milky Way

If We

If we knew it all, we would never have any questions to ask.

Jesus knows it all.

Many people don't believe.

If we could do all things, there would be nothing left to be done.

Jesus can do all things for you and me.

If we could see what everybody is doing, then no criminals would ever get away with a crime.

God sees everybody in every neighborhood that is not good.

If we could hear what everybody says, there would be no silence.

God can hear us all every day.

God can silence anyone to listen to him.

If the Lord gives us everything that we ask him for, then we will take Jesus too lightly.

Jesus may not answer all of our prayers.

If we were all wise, we would need no laws to correct foolishness like Jesus was up against when He lived in this world.

Jesus was all-wise to always rebuke sin.

Life Can't Promise Us

Life can't promise us that things will always be easy to do.

Jesus has promised us hope in Him for you and me to cope in this life.

Life can't promise us that this world won't bully us with its troubles.

We can trust Jesus to protect our souls from being lost if we make him our choice.

Life can't promise us that we will live to see another day.

Jesus will promise you and me eternal life if we are saved in him who has no end in life.

Life can't promise us that life will always be nice to us; life can sometimes be mean.

Jesus Christ, Our Lord, is always so nice to you and me.

Life can't promise us a good time all the time because life can burden us down to not find our true calling. Jesus will always call us to come to Him with our burdens.

Life can't promise us that the sun will always shine in our lives.

Jesus can always make to shine no matter what we've been through and are going through to show and tell that Jesus is for us, that the devil will surely know.

The Cross

The cross has four sides to represent the north and south, and east and west sides of this world where every mouth can confess and repent of their sins unto Jesus Christ, whose arms were stretched out on the cross that he paid our price on for all souls to come to him.

The cross has four sides to make a full circle for all to be saved and abide by His holy law.

The cross has four sides that Jesus shed His blood on to cleanse all men of their sins.

The cross has led many souls to be saved in Jesus, who hung on the cross to circle around the four corners of the world where you and I don't know all.

Those who truly believe in Jesus will be saved.

Jesus felt so much pain on every side of the cross on that memorable day that no Christian will ever forget.

Jesus died on the cross.

The cross has four sides for every eye to live by faith in Jesus, who didn't leave anyone out.

Many will doubt they won't be saved on the four corners of the cross.

To represent Jesus, we must die to self to live a renewed life in Jesus, who rose from the grave that is powerless to the cross that will live on throughout eternity.

Can Cause

A trick can cause us to believe that it must be true.

Jesus will never trick us to believe in him all through our lives.

A wish can cause us to want something good or bad to happen.

Jesus is real above any wish that we can dish out.

A smile can cause us to feel good without a doubt.

Jesus can give us joy to be like a little child playing with his toys.

A runner can run for miles and miles.

Jesus has given us a race to run to win the prize of eternal life in Him, who will come back again up in the sky.

Our eyes can cause us to look up and down and all around.

We can see Jesus in all good things, with that we can never disagree.

A beautiful woman can cause a man to lose himself in her beauty.

Jesus can find him and bring him back to himself.

We can cause a friend to not be a friend if we are dishonest.

Jesus is always honest with us

He is a friend we can always trust.

Being in love can cause us to feel like we are on top of the world to catch a falling star.

Love is God, who is always the first one to love us and wants us to one day be with him beyond the stars.

Community Service

When Jesus lived on earth, he did community service work.

He fed the hungry and spoke words of Truth that didn't hurt their hearts.

Jesus healed the sick and cast demons out of many people in the community.

Jesus was all about loving people and saving their souls.

Jesus was completely selfless in helping people in the community that he lived in and was a genuine friend to those in need.

The Pharisees and Sadducees had questioned Jesus's community service work. They felt it was a bad thing for their ministry, which was a no good ministry to the people they wanted to believe in them.

Jesus has given you and me community service work to do for His holy name's sake and not in our names.

This whole world is our community, where Jesus loves all the same. We all have a need of something for our good.

Jesus Christ our Lord is the greatest community service worker, and we should always love and trust Him to supply all of our needs. Jesus is our greatest community service leader. With this, no Christian can disagree.

I am Your Mirror

One day I didn't want to look in the mirror because my eyes were full of tears because the Lord showed me how I was so guilty of hurting others who he'd given up his life to save.

I asked the Lord, "What do you want me to do?"

The Lord gave me my answer by saying, "I am your mirror, for you to look in and see me without sin and to cleanse you of your sins."

That can't reflect on Me because I am your mirror.

You can look at me and see yourself belonging to me and not you.

I am your Lord, who is your mirror on the wall of your heart.

I will never smear you up or ever break all through your life, that can break into pieces if you choose to not reflect Me by not keeping My laws in your heart.

You can look into a lot of mirrors, but I am Jésus Christ, your only mirror that will show your heart's flaws and sins to reflect on man-made mirrors below the heavens.

To Forgive is to Heal

To forgive is to heal emotionally, and let go the pain no matter how long that pain has been there upon our name.

When to forgive is to heal insane feelings that can make the mind and body ill because holding grudges will sooner or later make us sick in some kind of way, especially spiritually sick day after day.

To Forgive is to heal the hurt and make it go away.

We need to forgive to free our hearts of so much pain that we can engrave in our heart by holding it in because of our pride.

That can surely lie to us and make us believe that it's right to not Forgive, when Jesus said to his Father, "O Lord, forgive them for they know not what they do."

That's what Jesus expressed from his heart to save me and you.

You and I Can Control

The wind cannot control its blow, when you and I can choose to control our tongues that blow so free and strong.

Like the wind over the ocean waters that can't control their flow, when you and I can choose to control our actions to not overflow and flood on one another.

We can choose to control what we say and what we do because of our God-given free will choice day after day. Choose not to say chilling words and not to do chilling things.

The land cannot control natural disasters, but you and I can choose to control the way that we live so as to not be a disaster to God's golden rules that won't control us and make us obey God.

Any normal, mature person can choose to control their mind to think on doing God's will all the time because of our free will choice under the sunshine.

We Will Be Eternal One Day

We will be eternal one day if we are saved in Jesus Christ, who will one day raise the righteous dead from their graves and change the righteous living from mortal to immortality.

You and I will one day be eternal for holding onto Jesus through the pain and suffering of this life that is temporary under the sun.

Jesus Christ is eternal, beyond the sun. He will make us eternal one day in the new heaven and earth, while the wicked will pass away one day like they never lived in this world where sin leads to death, while salvation in Jesus leads to eternal life.

In the end, we will be eternal and get the victory to win.

Music Was Originated

Music was originated to give God the glory and praise because God is the ancient of days.

Music began in heaven when Lucifer was a great singer and a great musician above all the other angels.

Before his great fall from heaven, where his music was originated for God's pleasure.

God is before and after all that he created and his creations enjoy giving Him songs of worship and praise in the highest.

This is inspiration that sin cannot deteriorate because music was originated to magnify and honor God, who loves me and you every day.

God loves gospel music. Do Him good and right so he blesses our souls and we can be saved by his Son, who the heavenly angels behold.

The King of

The sun is the king of the sky, with its white carpet of clouds rolled out across the four corners of the world. It shines so proud beneath the universe. It is the king of the solar system.

We bow down unto the eternal light high above the gravity that keeps our feet on the ground.

That is the king of the earth, where the streets are the king of the cities and towns all around. That life is the king of every living creature.

Death is the king of the grave, where the dead can't do anything under the sun.

Our choice is the King of our destiny. We all do have to bring God's judgment upon our hearts, so all know that Jesus Christ is the King of eternal life in heaven, where we want to go one day.

Today, we must make Jesus the King of Kings in our hearts.

We must bow down and worship Jesus Christ from the start to the end of our lives.

The things of this world will lose their crowns and step down from the throne of our hearts.

We choose to love Jesus, who is the king of the golden rules that we will keep. If we love Jesus so very true, we will have life eternal.

Can't Get Rid of God

A man can get rid of some bad evidence so it won't be used against him in court where we can go for good or bad.

A man or woman can get rid of a spouse by divorce. That can be a hard thing to understand in this world.

A fool can't get rid of God, even if he believes that there is no God. We don't see God with the naked eye, but we can feel his presence being so divine wherever we go to and fro.

Through the earth, that can't get rid of the sky, where Jesus Christ will one day soon be seen by every eye in the land of the living.

You can't get rid of God, who is always giving his mercy and grace to all great and small.

God can't get rid of His laws that point out our sins, He will one day get rid of those lost in this world that will pass away.

Those who don't love and obey his Son, Jesus Christ, will be faced with the devil. The devil, who failed when Jesus rose from the grave giving us victory over death and hell.

If you Want to Know

If you want to know what is missing in your life, study the bible. Doing that will let you and me know about the Lord Jesus Christ, who we can't afford to miss out on in our lives.

Many people travel around the world trying to find what is missing in their lives.

The devil values this.

No matter who we are or where we live, in this fallen world if you want to know what is missing in your life, study the bible.

Doing that will give you the right answers when you and I need them.

We must know that if we miss out on Jesus, we will never find anything worth being at the top of our list of life.

Only Jesus Christ can always fulfill our needs.

No matter where we go, here and there, the bible is always real.

It gives you and me Jesus, who will give us what we are missing under all the falling stars.

We were created in God's image, to choose to come back to Jesus, who always sees us missing what he offers to us in his Holy word that many people don't believe.

Great All By Himself

Only God is great all by Himself, while you and I need the approval of many people to make us great.

We human beings cannot make that great accomplishment on our own. That will not make you or me a great person in this big wide world that God created.

He is a great God all by himself. He moves our hearts to repent of our sins and give Him all the glory and praise to be a great thing to do day after day.

You and I cannot make ourselves great.

It will take many people to see and believe that you and I have a great gift to uplift them and change their lives for the better.

In a world of dim and grim hope, only God can give to all men through His Son, Jesus Christ.

No one will ever be greater than Him under and beyond the sun that shines its light so great over all the world.

Only God is great by Himself. He gave us his only begotten Son to put an end to all sin that will cause great loss to many souls.

We will miss out on heaven if we don't humble ourselves before the Lord.

Choose to love Jesus Christ, who is great without our approval, because not loving Him will mean missing out on eternity.

A Witness of Jesus

The beautiful green grass, flowers and trees are witnesses of Jesus for us to see wherever we go from state to state and from country to country.

The dry land is a witness of Jesus giving all and not just some piece of dry land to live on. That land shows us so well.

The sky is a witness of Jesus Christ, for the sky tells us that Jesus will not touch down on the earth when he comes back again for every eye to see him up in the sky.

Life is a witness of Jesus, for life tells us that we haven't licked the dust because life can trust Jesus, who let us live to see this day that He gives to us for free.

All the elements of the earth are a witness of Jesus, for the elements tell us that Jesus put them there for us to use, no matter where we live.

Time is a witness of Jesus Christ, and tells us that today is our time to choose to live for Jesus or live for self.

Time can't choose for us who's time is overdue.

Death is a witness for the devil, for death tells us that the devil doesn't care anything about what level of education we have; it doesn't impress him.

He will destroy us all and make us go to hell if we don't know Jesus.

Jesus gives us salvation, so be a witness of Jesus and know life after death.

In the Blood

Life is in the blood that every human being and animal must have to live upon the land where life is not in the things that we possess from the north, south, east and west side of this world.

Life is in the blood running through our veins. We're all the same, no matter what our name is.

Only the blood of Jesus Christ can cleanse us all, great and small, from our sins,

Jesus Christ's blood is the only blood that was shed for us to receive eternal life.

It's Jesus's blood that floods life eternal into all who believe in Him.

Jesus Christ will save you and me through his precious blood that has the power to give us life to live so we can reach an old age that we don't deserve because we pollute our own blood and shorten our lives like a bird landing into a grease pit, and may never fly again in the sky under the highest heaven above.

Our lifeblood can't renew life for us. To deny self is to be cleansed in the blood of Jesus, who has no stains of sin before our eyes.

Make Jesus Look Good

Do we make Jesus look good before one another or do you and I try to make ourselves look good before others?

To believe that we are looking so good with what the Lord has given to us is selfishness before the Lord each and every day.

We can be so busy making ourselves look good for others that we can't see Jesus Christ in our attitudes and body language.

That can turn our hearts away from Jesus, who loves every man, woman, boy and girl.

We should make everyone look good for loving and obeying Him like we should always do in this world where life is too short to not make Jesus look good.

The angels in heaven will exhort Jesus Christ to be the King of Kings and Lord of Lords, beyond you and me.

Don't make yourself look so good in sinning against God. Our pride will only grow thorns to God.

The Rocks are Preaching the Truth

The rocks are preaching the truth about the bible being so true.

There are many skeptics who believe the bible to be a lie.

So many archaeologists are proving that the stories in the bible are real, and the rocks that are being dug up tell a reliable story about many ancient prophets of God and Kings that existed according to the bible scriptures.

This is what preachers will cling to.

The oldest preacher is in the rocks, preaching the truth to many archaeologists, who are receiving true evidence that got buried thousands of years ago.

The Lord kept the Dead Sea Scrolls in good condition so they could be read today in agreement with bible scriptures that will not go void.

The rocks preach about the bible being so true from the ground up to the heavens looking down and rejoicing.

The rocks cry out to us and tell us that God cannot lie to even the rock. They are preaching the truth to many archaeologists.

The rocks will not deny the bible's truth, below the heavens on high.

In the Family of God

I don't see black and I don't see white in the family of God, who is always right about what He says in His holy word that is for everyone to live by.

I don't see skin color under the sun.

When it comes to anyone who loves the Lord Jesus Christ who gave his life to save all men who live a Christian life.

I love to see that.

No matter the color of the skin. It doesn't matter to the Lord, who hates our sins.

Sins have no color to God, who sees all men being a sinner in His holy presence.

There is no color barrier in being saved in God's grace. God gives to all who will face his judgment one day.

The family of God is one spiritual race of people who Jesus sweetly embraces to save.

It's How We Handle Our Blessings

When the Lord blesses us, it's how we handle our blessings that count. We can't let it go to our heads.

That's what will happen if you and I are filled with self-pride. The Lord hates that.

We should handle our blessings with humility.

This is what we need to give to the Lord Jesus Christ every day.

He blesses us in many ways that we can handle if we don't take the Lord's blessings for granted.

We can unawarely be unthankful and close the door of our hearts against the Lord in some kind of way.

If we mishandle our blessings from the Lord, even this very day, then we don't deserve to be blessed.

The Lord will never say a wrong word to us and will never do us wrong because His blessings are always right for us.

We can surely miss out on a blessing from the Lord if we don't handle our blessings with giving God the glory and praise to be seen in his power.

Jesus Walked with Me

Before I knew the Lord, I walked down a dark spiritual road that the Lord walked with me though I didn't know it.

I just didn't know that Jesus guarded my soul as I walked down that road to hell.

That's where I was going and I didn't care to know until Jesus opened my eyes.

On that spiritually dark road I didn't see any light of God's word shining all around me.

I believed I was right about the way I lived my life, even though it was about to destroy me.

If Jesus had left me all alone down that dark road where he gave me a second chance to wise up and walk down the straight and narrow road, I would've been lost.

God's truth set me free. I am so glad that Jesus Christ, my Lord and savior, molded me and shaped me in his love.

I obey Him who shines his holy light all through the dark spiritual road.

Jesus walked that road with me, even though I didn't have a clue.

When I was Living in Darkness

When I was living in darkness, it was like heaven on earth to me.

That darkness looked to be so right and so good in my eyes.

I was too blind to see the light of the world shining in God's love all around me.

When I lived in darkness it was like heaven on earth to me who had loved darkness like it was my first girlfriend who I truly adored and loved to be with.

Today, I love living in the Truth that set me free from my dark past life because now I see the light of the world in the bible.

It reveals the bright morning star to me in my repentant heart unto my Lord Jesus Christ, the Son of God.

He is shining through my soul and I am saved from being lost in the darkness that I had loved and embraced as if it were my true soul mate that Jesus replaced.

No One Can Get Higher Than God

No angel can get higher than God — the fallen angels found that out the hard way. This is true all around the eternal heavens.

No human being can get higher than God. King Nebuchadnezzar found this out in the wilderness so far apart from civilization.

We can't get higher than God, who's the highest of the highest life, love, peace and joy throughout the heavens above the earth.

No creature and no material things can get higher than the Son of God, who is the King of Kings beyond opinions and theories.

You can't get higher than God, who proves fools to be so wrong across every land and sea.

Death can't get higher than God, who created eternal death for lost, unrepentant souls to burn in hell.

None can get higher than God, who's higher than all visible and invisible things in heaven and on earth.

God's laws are eternal to keep because God's holy law is God, who cannot fall down below his character that is higher than eternal life beyond this flawed, sinful world.

The Church is Moving

The church is moving in the direction of heaven like the clouds move across the sky so quiet. The clouds can move in different directions according to what direction the wind blows.

The church will move you and me in only one direction — to heaven. There is no other direction to get there.

Jesus Christ is the living wind that blows our souls across his great blue skies of salvation for all, great and small, to be in his church.

In the winter, spring, summer and fall the church is moving in the direction of heaven, where Jesus Christ will come to fill the sky with eternal light and eternal life to give to his church bride and take her to heaven one day soon.

No fallen angel and no lost human being will move to heaven beyond the moon, sun and stars. They are moving in the direction of hell.

The church is moving in the direction of heaven above because of Jesus Christ, who is moving God's love in the direction of sinners who need to be saved.

Right Now

My Lord Jesus Christ give me strength right now to resist the devil's temptations that he loves to dish out to me. I need you, my Lord Jesus, right now.

That seems so eternal with You who eternity loves to hang around forever and ever.

Right now You are my higher bound, O Lord for me to reach up with my heart of repentance unto You who is right now and forever more.

The love of God is all around my soul that needs to be saved in You right now.

My Lord Jesus, who is faithful and true to me right now this very moment that I am alive because of you O Lord. I need You to keep Your eyes on me.

Right now I would be foolish to live by my eyesight when right now I need to keep my faith in You, who is the light of the world shining through this dark world.

Right now save me from my sins.

Right now I will choose to follow You, for if I chose to follow the world You would show mercy on me right now.

Working It Out

We shouldn't look at the bad situations that we are in when we should trust Jesus who is working it out for you and me.

We can't always work out our problems on our own.

We can try and fail and end up being left all alone with the bad situation getting the best of us.

We need to always let Jesus work it out for us, since we can mess up things on any day.

If we go it alone, we will end up regretting not waiting for the Lord to help us work it out.

He will help us work it out as we sleep the night away.

More and more of our blessings will come our way if we put things in His hands, relying on Your promise that you will never break.

The Lord will work it out on time and never, ever be too late to come through for you and me.

Surely you know that the Lord Jesus Christ is so good to us from head to toe.

The Lord is Always Ahead of Us

The Lord is always ahead of us. We can never leave the Lord behind us, so we can never get ahead of the Lord.

We believe with all our mind and heart that the Lord is always ahead of us and will never fail us. We can trust Him every day.

The Lord Jesus Christ is ahead of us and moves the obstacles that he foresees in our past present and future.

He has to be ahead of us, because we can sometimes leave ourselves behind the truth that He gives to us.

We have to believe to stay ahead of the devil's lies that can never get ahead of the Lord, who is greatly alive and not dead.

The Lord is always ahead of life and death, to give you and me a second chance to get our hearts right with Him.

He is always ahead of us to never leave us out of his eyesight.

God is God in Nature

God is God in nature, which represents the presence of God in our eyesight.

We see the peace of God in nature from the start of the day to the end of the day.

God is God in nature, and shows us His love for us in nature everywhere we go.

To see God in nature that won't deny there is a God who lives even in nature.

Nature does God's will, just as we need to do so real.

Nature worships God in its still, quiet voice, and God hears beyond our ears that need to be filled with God's Word.

God is in nature all around the world. Nature knows God to be holy and righteous and all-loving.

Nature beholds and is a good example to teach you and me to search for God with all of our hearts and find God in nature, in His word and in the church.

God's Son is the head of God's holy ministry work.

In this Sinful World

I don't want to live forever and ever in this sinful world.

Only Jesus Christ could come and get the power over sin.

Jesus alone was living eternally without sin.

If you and I could live forever with sin, there would be no hell for no one to go to because there would be no end to sin.

God hates sin forever and won't allow sin to go on forever in this world.

I don't want to live forever in sin, for I would rather die than have sin be all right with me.

I am saved in Jesus Christ and will not live forever in this sinful world.

Many people would like to live forever in their sins in this sinful world.

They will never repent unto the Lord who lives forever without sin all through His ancient days.

I want to live doing right by the Lord.

You and I could live forever in this world of sin, but the Lord will one day destroy to not let sin be around forever.

The devil is always at the door of God's grace.

The devil wishes he had the power to keep that door open because he wants to live forever in his sins.

God's grace will not be forever upon you and me to be saved and be set free from living in sin that the devil doesn't want to see.

God is so merciful to not let you and me live in this sinful world forever.

Who Else Can I Talk to Better?

Who else can I talk to better than talking to my Lord?

I can talk to Him with all of my heart and never get bored at any time or anywhere.

I can't talk to anyone else, because they could never show me all of myself like my Lord Jesus Christ can.

I can always talk to Him about anybody and anything.

He comforts me without a doubt, and I know I am always talking to the right One.

Who else can I talk to better than you O Lord?

No one else can out reason and out do You or rise above You, Lord.

You have the right answers to give to me.

Who can talk big when it's small talk to you?

You show me how small-minded I can be before you O Lord.

You are always the best one to help me see my true self.

The Lord can never run out of the right words to say to you and me. I know He will not run out of the right words to say to me every day.

I can Only Trust the Lord

I can't trust my own eyes to always see what I need to see to bless my eyes.

I can't trust my own ears to always hear what I need to hear to bless my ears so dear.

I can't trust my own tongue to always say what I need to say in love to bless my tongue day after day.

I can't trust my own hands to always do what I need to do to bless my hands all through the day.

I can't trust my feet to always walk where I need to walk to bless my walk doing good deeds for the Lord.

I can't trust my own heart to always be real and true to bless my heart.

I know that Jesus will never deceive me because I can only trust my Lord Jesus Christ to always do me right to bless my life.

The Seat Belts of My Life

Only You, O Lord, can fasten the seat belts of my life and save my soul in the vehicle of your grace.

You spare my life to face up to the road-ragers of disappointment that tries to run me off Your straight and narrow road.

O Lord, I know you will take control of the steering wheel of my heart if I always choose You to help me start my day off.

You drive my desires in the lane of a long spiritual drive, taking my heart to love you, O Lord, every day.

Only You, Lord Jesus Christ, can fasten the seat belts of my life when my hands are broken in sin that will throw me through the windshield of the uncertain, making me land down hard in spiritual trauma to my soul.

Only You, O Lord, can heal me and let me go on driving in your spirit. You lead me to your road to heaven.

Your Holy Spirit, O Lord

Your holy spirit, O Lord, is amazing to remind me of things that I need to say and do.

Your holy spirit, O Lord, shows me things I need to see so clear when Your holy spirit brings me peace of mind and comforts me in my distress.

O Lord, You give me your holy spirit to help me to express what is in my heart.

Your holy spirit convinces me to confess and repent of my sins.

The truth will set me free.

My Lord Jesus, Your holy spirit teaches me all truth about who I need to be in my life every day.

Your holy spirit, O Lord, is amazing and so nice to always remind me that you, O Lord, paid my price.

We Can Have No Idea

We can have no idea how the Lord can bless us.

We often have no clue about how the Lord will test us to trust Him in uncertain situations that can easily come about any day.

We can have no idea about how we can doubt the Lord, who can bless us even in unknown ways that we don't see.

We have no idea about what the Lord may or may not do for us today. The Lord can use us to bless one another if we do what he says.

The Lord makes a way out of no way.

We can have no idea about what the Lord will do for us.

It can be so real and a blessing that we may not see coming our way.

We can have no idea about what the Lord has for us.

We cannot say enough words and cannot do enough good things unto the Lord.

We receive his blessings and learn more and more about God's goodness to us.

Everybody Has a Presence

Everybody has a presence to be seen by people in this world.

We are seen by the living whose sins are always present.

The Lord Jesus Christ is always present and lived a life without sin when he walked this earth.

A baby has a presence to cry out loud in its crib and be heard by its parents.

The parents have a presence to be seen by their children day after day.

God sees everybody who is present and God is present when our naked eyes can't see Him.

He can do all things beyond and below the sky because God has a presence to never end.

Our own heart can end its presence in the grave that is present before God.

He will one day raise the righteous dead in Jesus Christ our Lord, who is present in heaven forever and ever more.

Heaven is Drawing Nearer

Heaven is drawing nearer to all who have been born again in Jesus Christ our Lord and savior, who died for our sins and rose from the grave.

Heaven is drawing nearer to all who are saved in Jesus, who wants to save the great and small around the world.

Heaven is drawing nearer to all the saints who will not faint in times of trouble that we will go through.

We will be saved in Jesus' name if we love him and obey Him who created heaven and earth.

Heaven is drawing nearer to the end of this world.

All who are redeemed will one day go with Jesus to heaven above this dark, sinful world.

Many hearts will wax cold and have no love for Jesus Christ, the Son of God who is in heaven.

Heaven is drawing nearer to hearts of repentance who follow Jesus Christ, who will be greatly applauding all of his holy children when they're accepted into heaven.

Heaven is drawing nearer to our days of the midnight, morning and afternoon.

Over Temporary Things

So many people are wasting their lives away over temporary things that will pass away one day when Jesus Christ comes back again like the bible says.

Temporary things are not worth more than our souls that are so precious to the Lord who created all things seen and unseen.

So many people have lost their souls over temporary things that are of no value to the Lord, who has eternal things to give to you and me if we truly and greatly live our lives doing His holy will that is written in His holy word so real.

Jesus is real over temporary things that will leave our souls so empty day after day.

Jesus is never a waste of our time.

We should all fill our lives with spiritual things to season our hearts like a beautiful warm day in the spring.

My Spirit is Willing

My flesh is weak to sin, but my spirit is willing to do the Lord's will day after day.

My flesh is weak to give into the lust of this world, but my spirit is willing to trust the Lord each and every day.

The Lord loves all of us who are born in sin.

God hates sin, but loves our souls and will save them from the weakness of the flesh that loves to get the best of us day after day.

My spirit is willing to call on the Lord Jesus Christ and ask him for strength to go through this life of wicked enticements that won't leave us alone.

I will get closer and closer to my Lord, who owns my flesh and my spirit day after day.

The Holy Spirit longs for my soul to be saved in Jesus, who is beyond my flesh and my spirit. I look up to him from sun up to sun down.

The Lord can make my spirit strong over my weak flesh that's been upon me for so long.

To Uplift Jesus' Name

You and I just don't know when we'll have to help someone to get through the day under the sky so blue.

We can lift up Jesus' holy name by lending someone a helping hand to make their day a good day under the sun that shines down on sinners and saints.

The saints of God know that it's good to bless people's lives with the love of Jesus in our hearts, uplifting Jesus' holy and precious name because it's the right thing to do for a Lord who has no blame of sin.

You and I are blamed for sin in many ways but we can uplift Jesus' holy name throughout the day.

It's always good to love one another in Jesus' name.

That will always make demons tremble and make you and me real about being aware of our sinful condition.

Each of us should know that the name of Jesus is all-powerful to and fro, throughout the land of the living.

We were born to uplift Jesus' name all around the world. Jesus is a gift to us all.

I Must Walk Alone

I must walk alone to examine myself to be like Jesus or not like Jesus.

For me to truly see, I must walk alone through my days and my nights

I may be surrounded by uncertainty, but Jesus is my light.

I walk alone with him in His truth that will set me free from lies that love to get in my way.

I must walk alone to the cross to pick up my cross all alone and follow Jesus, who will stick closer by me than my mother, father, sister or brother.

There is no other to walk with me as I repent of my sins unto Jesus Christ, my Lord who gave me a free will choice so I could choose Him.

I walk all alone on the course to salvation that Jesus alone can give to me. I will not be lost.

You Are

You are before me and you are after me, O Lord, who are the ancient of days before I was ever born into this world.

You are after me when I die after my short life under the stars.

My three score in ten days can be only lengthened by you, my Lord Jesus Christ, who was before Abraham and after Abraham.

Because you are the Lamb of God, You are before me and after me.

My life is like a shadow, fading away in the daylight and in the night.

You are before me and after me into a thousand years being like yesterday to You, O Lord, who are so dear to my life.

You let me live to see this day and that you are before me and after me in every way under the sun and beyond the sunny rays.

Jesus Will Never Fail

Jesus will never fail you and me, even though we can fail to say some words that we need to say.

You and I can fail in what we need to do, especially for the Lord, who will never fail to be there for us.

He will be there when we need him the most, and that can happen on any day that we can fail to boast about Jesus Christ before the world from coast to coast.

Jesus will never fail all who love him with all their hearts.

What can fail you and me is deceiving ourselves and starting our days off not trusting in Jesus to bring us through.

We have failed more than a few times, but Jesus can use that to make us strong in Him day by day.

Jesus will never fail you or me when we pray to God, who is always very near and not far away.

There Is No Way Out

There is no way out of being tempted for as long as we live.

There is no way out of doing something wrong and not getting away with it.

God does things so right all the time, and there is no way out of God's eyesight seeing every right and wrong thing that you and I do.

There is no way out of God's judgment upon our hearts.

God will judge us according to his ten commandments that we can't leave out of our daily lives.

There is no way out of sin. Sin will not give us a way out of our souls being lose in hell if we go against God's will.

There is no way out of being saved, if we trust Jesus, who never fails us.

There is no way out of our trials, but Jesus makes a way out for you and me to be spiritually awake and saved.

Cannot Flatter

Evil cannot flatter good that knows no evil deeds and no evil words that Jesus will never do or say to you and me.

Hate cannot flatter love and make it give in to hate.

Foolishness cannot flatter wisdom and make it give into foolishness.

No human being can flatter God and make him give into the sinful nature of man. God cannot lie and cannot die.

Injustice cannot flatter justice and make it turn a blind eye to injustice. Jesus is all about treating people right and giving all a fair trial in his judgment every day and every night.

Slavery cannot flatter freedom.

No one will be put into slavery when living for Jesus.

He is freedom from living in sin that breaks the rules of freedom.

Strife cannot flatter peace. Jesus gives us peace to get a good night's sleep if we keep our minds on Him who is the prince of peace.

Will I follow the Crowd or Will I Stand Alone?

Will I follow the crowd or will I stand alone and not bow down to the god of this world who is the prince of darkness.

I am convinced to do what the Lord says day after day in every way?

If I follow the crowd down the road to destruction, I can't blame anyone but myself, who Jesus will burn up in His eternal flames.

I could lose my life and one day soon find the treasures of everlasting life .

I could easily follow the crowd of the devil right in the church, but Jesus has given me a choice to stand up for Him, who died on the cross.

Will I follow the crowd or will I stand all alone for Jesus, up against even those who I so dearly love the most from head to toe?

The choice is mine. I must make it all alone.

Will I follow the crowd or make my stand for Jesus?

Jesus is making reservations for me to bow down and worship Him around His holy throne. Of course, I choose Him.

Belongs to the Lord

There are many shootings going on in the schools because of murderers falling through the cracks and no background checks on their mental health.

Every human being's body and breath belongs to Jesus, who has the right to give life and take it away.

Our lives are meant to be lived for Him.

There are some shootings going on in the church that anyone can come to and repent of their sins before the Lord and before the church.

Everyone belongs to Jesus, whether being in the schools or being in the church.

It's wrong to take anyone's life.

That life belongs to the Lord, who will punish murderers.

They will truly feel his wrath in the jail cell that is filled with criminals.

When a criminal gives his life to Jesus, he is saved but will still have to pay for his crimes here on earth. Jesus wouldn't disagree with that at any time.

One Thing in Common

Being real and pretending has one thing in common — both can get our attention.

Each and every day when it comes to food it can be sweet or sour.

The one thing these have in common is that both have a taste.

A Christian and an atheist have one thing in common — both have a fate.

The rich man and poor man have one thing in common — Jesus owns them both and is their king of kings.

A human being and an animal have one thing in common — they both have a soul like the bible says.

What we say and what we do only have one thing in common — both have language and are so real in this world Jesus lived in, speaking both languages without ever sinning against God.

Jesus Will Always Know

You and I will usually know when something just doesn't seem to be right, so we're not sure when Jesus knows everything and brings that one thing to our attention that we need to know.

You and I will usually know when our enemies are around because they will talk loud in their body language that will give them away.

We will usually know when our friends are around because they will help us to feel better if we are feeling down.

Jesus Christ always knows our enemies and our friends because He knows the heart of everyone who He lends borrowed time to.

You and I will usually know if something is wrong with our loved ones we've known for a long time.

Jesus will always know when something is wrong with every one of us and He will never overlook anyone from sun up to sun down.

There are Mosquito People

There are mosquito people who can bite us with their words and with their actions and can cause us to itch with doubts about them not being Christians, even though they go to church and clap their hands.

Mosquitoes will surely suck our blood out of our veins, and mosquito people will suck away our innocence away and make us feel guilty about the conclusions they draw about us.

Without a doubt the devil's temptations are spiritual mosquitoes trying to suck out our spiritual walk with the Lord.

God's word is our spiritual mosquito repellent and it protects us from the mosquito bites of the devil.

A mosquito can buzz in our ears to make a sound that's so annoying, but Jesus will kill spiritual mosquitoes with his truth on his holy ground.

A mosquito bite can surely itch and it can spread, but Jesus can stop the spiritual itch and keep it from spreading in the church among his sheep.

Mosquitoes can carry the West Nile virus, but Jesus can carry the cure to get rid of spiritual itch and make our hearts pure.

There is No Weight

There is no weight to a fly that can land on us, who may not know it.

Our tongue can carry a weight of words to knock someone down on the ground of hatred.

The holy bible will carry a heavy weight of the truth that is always reliable to lead us to Jesus, who has no weight of sins.

There is no weight to the air that we breathe and there is no weight in our eye vision to see.

You and I can blow hot air in the form of words and create a heavy weight of strife.

The truth of God's word has no heavy weight on anyone who lives his or her life by the truth that is light like the air to anyone being set free by the truth.

There is no weight to a feather that can float through the air. Jesus can float our minds on the air of his peace.

There is no weight in a bubble that will burst so silent in the air. We should love Jesus first because He wants to burst our bubbles of selfishness.

Life's Best Friend

Love is our best friend because God is love and God is life throughout eternity in heaven above this world that can be so full of self.

Jesus is completely selfless to always give us a good deal in life. That gives life joy.

Life will never get enough of love when life and love have a bond like a husband and wife.

Jesus loves us to live our life in Him who paid our price.

We can be so thankful to Jesus that love is life's best friend because without love it would be so worthless to live in this sinful world below the heavens.

An Island

An island has a voice for all seamen to hear, calling them to come to it.

There is no fear of making its voice to be heard day after day, and year after year.

An island will sit all by itself in the sea where the island can look so free.

A man can sit all by himself and be in bondage of burdens as if he is less fortunate than an island.

A man will create his own island in his heart if he believes that God doesn't exist.

Jesus Christ is the Son of God.

An island will stand up for its presence, but a man may not stand up for himself to be free upon the land.

A man is truly free in Jesus Christ, who created the islands to be so free while being surrounded by the seas.

Making Adjustments

Making adjustments can be a good thing to get us out of our old ways of doing things that we can't always trust to be good for us.

Making adjustments is not always so easy to do, especially if we are so adapted to only one kind of way of living all through our past days.

The best adjustment anyone can make in his life is to confess and repent and believe in Jesus Christ.

Jesus can surely help us to overcome what we are so adapted to. Jesus can use us to glorify Him so we surely know.

Making adjustments in life can be so challenging at times, especially if we don't know the outcome of how we will end up.

Jesus always knows from day to day and year after year that making adjustments in Jesus' name will never bend or break our will to sin against Him.

Run Away

No man can run away from himself.

No man can run away from working out his own soul's salvation.

No man can runaway from his flaws, no matter where he runs to.

No man can run away from God's law that sees all of us being sinners who need Jesus Christ to set us free.

No man can run away from his own heart. A man can condemn his own heart, but that's not what God will do.

No man can run away from his destiny. You and I will have to face up to our destiny.

Jesus is always fair to let us choose our fate.

To Swirl Up

Our desires can cause us to swirl up in a big ball of selfishness that can swirl up our sins even on God's holy ground.

The wind can cause dust to swirl up in a big ball for us to see.

Life's circumstances can cause us to swirl up in a big ball of uncertainty.

God's grace can cause our souls to swirl up in a big ball of time that we borrow from God, who takes no pleasure in scaring us into being saved.

Life can cause us to swirl up in a big ball of grudges, as if people owe us something all the time.

We can fall down and be lost in our sins, but Jesus can swirl us up in his big ball of goodness that has a barrel full of souls He's leading to repent.

Jesus Plans

We can have a good plan to accomplish something great, and it may happen before we know it.

When Jesus' plan can make a wish and a luck to look so small and can make our plans to receive a guilty verdict before him whose plans will never go sour.

We can make a plan to do something good and as soon as we get close to fulfilling our plans, something can interrupt our plans to go down the drain like water.

If the Lord has a plan for us, nothing can interrupt His plan. We can always trust Him to follow through for us.

The Lord will laugh at a fool's plan that will sooner or later cause him to regret what he's done.

We can plan our day, but if Jesus is not in it then things will be uncertain and we may not follow through.

God's plans will always follow through, no matter how we feel or what we say.

A Park

A park can't promise us that there will be no danger lurking around when we visit.

Jesus can promise us safety in the park of His salvation.

A park is a place where people can go and relax as well as a place where children can go and play, day after day.

The bible is a spiritual park for us to go to and relax our minds in the truth, day after day.

God's holy park is open all the time.

Many people love to go to the park with their dogs before it gets dark.

Jesus loves to go to the park of our hearts and be the Lord of lives.

There are squirrels climbing up the trees in the park.

When Jesus loves to climb up in our minds, so we think about Him and He gives us peace of mind in the park of our lives.

The park will always welcome you and me into its quiet place so we can relax and enjoy its view.

We shouldn't waste any time.

We should go to God's park and be bathed in His saving grace.

Are Built

Bridges are built to cross over deep waters underneath.

The bridge that we do trust to cross over when the greatest belief is to believe that we can always trust Jesus Christ to cross us over into a born again life in Him.

Ships and trucks are built to carry a heavy load.

A heavy load of burden can break you and me down spiritually.

We can have an oil spill of worries while walking on the straight and narrow road.

Only Jesus can carry our heavy load of burdens for us, but we must do His will.

His will never breaks down on us.

Airplanes are built to carry passengers.

You and I are passengers who are flying on the airplane of God's grace that lands down on the airstrip of this world every day.

Women are built to carry a baby in their wombs. Jesus will never see any guilt in a child being born out of wedlock.

We Can Think and Believe That We Are Something

It's so easy to think that we are something, but our bodies can let us know that we are nothing when sickness in the world strikes.

In this world it's so easy to feel so important when we make good accomplishments.

A heartache, though, can make you and me feel like nothing.

Anyone can believe they are great and look so proud, but life can let us know that we are nothing to death. It barks loud and bites hard, but we don't like to think about it.

It's so easy to think that we are something when everything is going good for us, but we can sink down like a ship and lose everything we have.

We can look like nothing, like the dust on a shelf that means nothing much.

We can think that we are something until something bad comes our way and makes us feel like nothing.

Even when we lay down to sleep and wake up feeling like nothing until something good happens to us.

If people put us up on a pedestal, we can get a swelled head and believe that we are something great.

We excel high above others and value our good names, but our good name will mean nothing good if we make a big mistake for others to see.

People can't wait to bring our name down to nothing in the news media and on TV.

Can Raise a Nation

Tension can rise up in a divided nation like the sun that rises in the morning to set up high in the sky from sunrise to sunset.

There would be no protest to come upon a nation if a nation's government was always pleasing to the people.

They would have nothing wrong to say about the government if this was the case.

If a nation was perfect, the media would have no power.

If no one watched and listened to the news that is not always good to watch, many people wouldn't know what is going on in their nation.

Many people love to watch bad news, so that's what the media will mostly show.

Big business in a nation is produced by hard working people.

No good employment and no good production can cause a business to go under.

A prestigious and powerful crime fighter in a nation can become corrupt with greed at any time of the day and night.

Poverty in a nation is not always caused by rich, selfish people. Natural disasters can bring on poverty and make it rise high.

If a nation of people live by eyesight, the invisible God will never be acknowledged because no one will believe that God is real.

If a nation put its hope and trust in people, a nation will fall into the cracks and potholes on the road of spiritual poverty.

God's laws are rich in love, while many laws in a nation will oppress people. God's law can raise a nation above all of its burdens.

Life Can Teach Us

Life can teach us what it means to mature the easy way or the hard way, whether we live in a city or in a small rural area.

Life can teach us experience we can take with us wherever we go, so we don't make the same mistakes over and over.

Life can teach us to sooner or later wise up and not drink from someone else's cup of rebellion in this world.

Life can teach us to know what it means to hold onto life when we are sick and not want to go to the grave where there is no life to live.

Life can teach us to give this world what we are made of that will sooner or later show and tell on who we are.

This life can teach us how far we have come because as long as we live, life can teach us something new and good about our Lord Jesus Christ who is the life eternal beyond this life here on earth.

Life can teach us that we can curse our own lives for not putting Jesus Christ first in our lives.

Life can teach us to live our new birth after being born again in Jesus.

The False Church

The church building is not the false church. Inside the building are true and false worshippers in the holy eyes of God.

Many church buildings are not open seven days a week.

God sees the heart to be true or false beyond our hands and feet that can do good work on the outward appearance that may not be true to God, who loves to see you and me come together day after day in his Son's holy name.

People can heal the sick and cast out demons in the church, but they may still be lost in sin for having a false church in their hearts.

No matter what church building we are in, we should all be loving Jesus and obeying His ten Golden Rules of God's everlasting truth.

The false church will never be a part of God's elect. God will elect true repentant and obedient hearts in every church building made by man.

There are true and false worshippers in every church and we can know the difference through God's holy word of eternal truth about His Son, Jesus Christ, even though the false church can appear to out-shine the true church.

Jesus is the head of the true church, without a doubt.

Many People Will

Many people will move away from their country, state, city or town where they grew up because many people love to live on the ground of prosperity and gain some financial wealth that no one can put down.

Many women are looked at as being weak because of being feminine.

Many men are looked at as bad boys because of being masculine.

God created feminine and masculine to remain in their correct gender.

Many people will pay time no mind and put time up on a shelf to collect dust until they get sick and need to find some time to get well again. Time is on no one's side.

If God wants to, He can unwind our biological clocks and makes them stock ticking.

Today many people have a good start in life and end up with a bad finish. They keep company with trouble that is no friend.

Many people will have a bad start in life and end up with a good finish. They keep company with the Lord as if He is in body form.

Only a few people will be real about examining themselves to surely know that Jesus Christ is real in their lives.

Many people will feel so proud for being so intelligent, creative and skillful, when they will overlook how to get in tune with their natural senses that don't foul anyone's conscious.

How Would We Know?

How would we know who is leading us to Jesus Christ or away from Jesus Christ if we don't study the bible for ourselves day after day?

The devil can rise up in the church.

How would we know if we don't have a relationship with Jesus from our head to our toes and always talk and walk in the Holy Spirit?

He will always show us the wicked one.

Many people are so intelligent in talking about Jesus Christ and are very knowledgeable with the scriptures, but their body language is far away from their words about Jesus Christ.

How would we know if we don't know God's word? How could we discern the good or evil in anyone?

How would we know if the Lord has stepped down from the pulpit for Satan to appear?

If our ways are bowed down on selfish ground with the eyes of our hearts closed by the temporary things in this world that will blind our spiritual eyes and keep them from seeing the King of Glory stepping down from the pulpit to be very close beside us.

To strengthen our trust in Him, Jesus suffers long with us from dusk to dawn.

We don't know that Satan will take the life out of us if Jesus permits him to do so for whatever reason.

We can't question or doubt Jesus Christ.

How would we know our destiny if we don't take the route to the bible so we can know?

Hungry For ...

Many people are hungry for love until they get it and misunderstand it. They take it for weakness.

Many people are hungry for money and will empty their loved one's bank account.

Many people are hungry for attention until they get it from the wrong person who won't just go away.

May people are hungry for control and if they can't get their way with someone, they give that person the cold shoulder.

Many people are hungry for sex and may not want sex from the one they're married to.

They will lay down within the same bed with someone else

Many people are hungry for fame and want to be a star.

The stars in the sky will always shine bright without media broadcasts to tarnish their light.

Only a few people are hungry for God's holy word, and not many people will study and live by it no matter where they live.

Our Way and Not the Lord's Way

If we do things our way and not the Lord's way, it will catch up with us.

To reap what we sow, like the bible says, we have to do it the Lord's way or we will sooner or later suffer for not following the Lord's perfect way. It will never fail us.

Lot's wife did things her way and that caused her to turn into a pillar of salt because she didn't obey the Lord.

You and I can do so wrong when we insist on doing things our way. We can make excuses to try to make ourselves feel like we're right.

The devil can't wait for that to happen so he can take us out of the land of the living.

Doing our own thing can bring on heartache and even death.

Doing things our own way can be of no good use for you and me.

Do things the Lord's way, His way is higher than the heavens.

The way of Lord Jesus is to save the lost, but our ways can cause our souls to be lost.

Doing our own thing is taking our free will choice too far, trying to make ourselves look good.

If we can always get our way and be so right and defend ourselves, insisting on doing it our way and not the Lord's way, we are going to lose in the end.

The Lord's way is selfless and never self-centered.

Our Lord Jesus set us free and we need to follow the Lord's way.

Bible Stories

The bible stories let us know where we come from and how we got to where we are today.

The bible stories let us know who we are and tell us we're no different from the people in the bible who were far from God in their evil ways.

A few were close to God and loved and obeyed Him with all of their hearts.

The bible stories let us know where we are going — to heaven or to hell. It is our free will choice to do or not do God's will.

The bible stories let us know that the people in the bible were real people.

The bible stories let us know where sin comes from and who can save us from those sins before the end of this world.

The bible stores let us know what is good and what is evil. God is good and the devil is evil upon the land.

The bible stories let us know that God created a woman for man to band around her.

Everyone has a Right

Everyone has a right to believe what they want to believe. No one has the right to force his or her belief on another person.

Everyone has a right to his or her opinion, even if no one agrees.

Everyone has a right to talk about what they want to talk about, and everyone has a right to doubt.

Everyone has a right to take the route that they want to take in life and everyone has the right to choose the words they want to say and who they say them to.

Everyone has a right to look at who they want to look at, and everyone has a right to do this or that.

Everyone has a right to think what they want to think and everyone has a right to blink and wink their eyes.

Everyone has a right to say yes to whoever they want to say yes to, and everyone has a right to say no to whoever they want to say no to.

Everyone has a right to be with who they want to be with, and everyone has a right to flee from trouble.

Everyone has a right to do good, and everyone has a right to do evil upon the land.

Everyone has a right to worship who they want to worship and what they want to worship.

Everyone has a right to rise up to prosperity and everyone has a right to love or hate.

God has a right to judge everyone.

The Bible Will Tell Us

The bible will tell us that there is a God, but atheists don't believe the bible to be true.

Atheists will deceive themselves, but they don't fool God.

We believe the universe was created by God, when the atheists believe that it originated from a big bang from afar.

Beyond what the bible tells us about God creating the universe, there is law and order in the universe where this planet earth resides.

The planet earth is respected by all the other planets.

The atheists don't respect God, who created all the planets.

The solar system will not reject law and order in outer space.

Human beings created in the image of God can break God's law and put a limit on God.

This is what the atheists do.

They say there is no God.

The atheists will make the big bang theory a God to worship in their hearts.

Nature is so divine compared to our sinful nature that breaks God's law and order.

There is law and order in the earth's gravity upon the land.

That gravity will keep us from floating up into the sky.

The bible will tell us about the law of God, and that is for everyone to keep in every place around the world.

The big bang theory has no gravity to keep our prayers from floating up to God, beyond the ozone layer.

Evolution will only exist in the minds of the atheists.

The universe will not claim it in all for its light years.

The atheists' time will run out before they reach the center of the universe where God also exists.

The atheists will trust their theories that can design a fantasy below the universe that God designed and gave it law and order of truth.

No theories can rise above and establish chance over the bible that tells us no lies.

Time is Winding Up Fast

Thinking fast is a good thing when your life is in danger.

It is important to think fast and stay alive to see another day.

Many people who live in the big cities will talk fast and walk fast, but are slow to walk away from trouble.

They think they can out talk death, which is fast to kill anyone

Many people who live in the country are fast to run into trouble for thinking slow.

Time is winding up fast for this world to end under the sign of the rainbow.

Thinking slow is a good thing, because a hasty person can think too fast and say and do something wrong and end up looking like a fool to you and me.

Talking fast can be a good thing to keep someone else from saying something that he or she may regret.

Walking fast can be a good thing when you need to cross the street in fast-moving traffic.

Walking too slow could cause someone to meet his fate when crossing the street too slowly.

Time is winding up fast in this world where many church folks are slow about trusting Jesus to be their friend.

Many church folks are fast about trusting this world to be their friend, when this world is running out of time so fast.

Go now to our reward that Jesus will give to all who love Him and obey Him.

Believe in Me and You Shall be Saved

Jesus says, "If you believe in Me you shall be saved."

Jesus didn't say that you must get rid of all your faults in this world before you can believe in Me.

If you and I had to get rid of all of our flaws to believe in Jesus, we would never get rid of them on our own.

Jesus would not have to do a background check on you or me to see if we are good enough to believe in Him to be saved.

Jesus Christ our Lord never had to form a meeting with his disciples to vote on souls to save to add to His church.

Jesus says you must repent of your sins unto Me and believe in Me to be saved by being born again and baptized in the name of the Father, Son and Holy Ghost.

Believing in Jesus is loving Jesus and keeping His holy laws from coast to coast.

Anyone will be saved for believing in Jesus Christ as long as they truly deny self, beyond question and comment about me and you.

Baptism, church membership, church positions and keeping the law of God can't save us from our sins. We must believe in Jesus Christ with all our hearts for Jesus to save our souls.

Jesus will never force anyone to choose to believe in Him. Many fallen, sinful creatures will believe in creatures and get deceived.

I Am

I am nobody to the world, but I am somebody to Jesus Christ, who came from heaven and lived a sinless life that he gave up for me as if I was the only sinner in this world.

I am a nobody, as if I don't exist at all, but I am somebody for Jesus to save as if everyone else has no sins to confess and repent unto the Lord.

I am a somebody for him to Love and want to save in this world that doesn't care about who I am to my Lord Jesus who sees me to be somebody to Him who's given me his truth to set me free from being lost in this world.

I would rather be a nobody to everyone than be a nobody to Jesus, who is somebody greater than man to me who is nobody in this world.

I don't care to be somebody great because I would rather be somebody to Jesus than to make a great name for myself in this world that can't save me from my sins.

Only Jesus Christ, my Lord and savior, can do that for me.

I can be somebody going to heaven one day soon, to live forever beyond this temporary world.

I am a nobody to you, but I am somebody to Jesus' all-seeing eyes.

Our Conscious

If we think bad thoughts and don't think that it's bad, we will embarrass our conscious. It will want to give up on us.

We shouldn't give our conscious a bad deal.

If we say bad words and don't care, we will insult our conscious and it will want to run away from you and me.

If we do bad things and don't feel guilty, we will shame our conscious and it will want to hide away from us for being so lame-brained.

If we blame others for our own mistakes and believe that we are so right, we will trouble our conscious into not wanting to cleave to us.

If we use people and act so innocent like we've done nothing wrong, we will ill our conscious and it will not want to aid our mind.

For as long as we see no need to stop using people and if we believe that we are better than others and feel proud about it, we will grieve our conscious and it will want to fall like a star and disappear.

If we set up traps for people to fall into and love it, we will disturb our conscious and it will not want to be a friend to us and serve us with good reasoning.

If we hurt people's hearts and don't have remorse or ask for their forgiveness, we will harm our conscious and it will want to divorce us from hearing its voice.

If we get revenge on others for doing us wrong and chew it up and swallow it down like it tastes so good, we will ban our conscious from wanting to help us make a moral decision.

If we believe that Jesus needs us to give Him our favor or approval for Him to bless or curse people, we will crush our conscious and it will not want to have anything to do with us.

If we believe that we know something that the Holy Spirit doesn't know and we act like we can lead the Holy Spirit to go with us and move upon our hearts, then we will murder our conscious and it will not yield to the Holy Spirit that teaches all truth eternally.

Young is Forever

Young is forever in a picture where no one will ever age, even when the picture begins to fade.

Every day, we get a day older — young is forever in a memory that no one can take away from youth to old age.

We don't know what a day will bring.

Young is forever in a dream where activities can be so real and no one can steal this away from us our in sleep.

Young is forever in a film.

Whether you're tall or short, big or slim, youth is forever in the heart. The body can't age that away no matter where we live.

Young is forever in childbirth.

Babies are born every new day upon the earth. Babies are born of the wombs of mostly young mothers.

Young is forever in heaven above.

We Can Listen

We can listen to the wind blowing and hear it telling us that it has a nature to blow day in and day out. The wind will not listen to us.

We must put our trust in the Lord, for that is who the wind trusts.

We can listen to music and hear its sounds telling us that it is sound and can affect our minds all the time. Music will not listen to us, either.

We must not sound like a bunch of complainers to the Lord.

His music is always divine and holy. He helps us fight and win our battles.

We can listen to the insects and hear a buzzing sound telling us that we will make a buzzing sound to the Lord on His holy ground.

If we are coming to church to put on a show, no one will listen.

We can listen to the natural sound of the water flow, and hear the water telling us that it is in its nature to flow so calm. The water will not listen to us.

If we know to do right by the Lord and don't do it, then we need to listen to our conscious and hear that sweet inner voice telling us so very dear that it's in a forever right attitude we need to live.

We need to make the right conscious choice so nice or our conscious will not listen to us, either.

If we don't make Jesus Christ our choice in the voice of our lives, then we are lost.

An Enemy Within

An enemy within the judicial system is a judge giving in to bribes and getting financial gain to run for a higher office to do favors for the rich and oppress the poor, innocent citizens with more and more unnecessarily strict laws.

An enemy within the political system is a politician who's greedy for power and will lower taxes for the rich and raise taxes for the poor, who are already burdened with bills.

An enemy within the home is a spouse or child being full of themselves, as if no one else lives in the house.

An enemy within the military is a military person selling top-secret information to another nation.

This person doesn't care if our nation hits rock bottom with debt.

An enemy within a neighborhood is a neighbor who despises other neighbors and doesn't care if they get through their hard times.

An enemy within the church is anyone who believes that they can save themselves through their works.

An enemy within your own heart is deceiving yourself into believing that there is no God who is love.

We don't believe to be an enemy when love will not pull friends apart.

Gone Beyond the Point of No Return

Many people have gone beyond the point of no return and can't come back to God, who will forever stand firm on His holy word.

If anyone dies and they are lost in sin, they have gone beyond the point of no return and can't be saved in God's Son, Jesus Christ, who rose from the grave and went back to heaven.

The destiny of many has gone beyond the point of no return in this fast-paced world where everyone chooses his own destiny through free will choice.

This has taken many young people to an early grave. They were too late and lost to loving and obeying the Lord.

Gone beyond the point of no return is something that everyone will not avoid if they put themselves first and above the Lord Jesus Christ who will not leave us or forsake us to die and not live again if our life is saved in Him before we die.

Gone beyond the point of no return is for only Jesus to always know. He knows whose hearts are not anointed by the Holy Spirit.

The outward appearance cannot hide you if you have not been saved.

The Lord sees who has gone beyond the point of no return so clearly.

When you and I have a God-given choice and can choose not to go beyond the point of no return.

We should not reject Jesus and His salvation below the heavens.

The Church is Not About the Creature

The church is not about the creature making a good name for himself. You have spots and blemishes of sin and are guilty in the eyes of the Lord.

The church is all about building up his kingdom for the holy angels to jump up and shout for joy.

The church is not about the creature who has sins to confess and repent of unto the Lord, whose golden rules are for the creature to keep every day.

The creature has a nature to sin against God, regardless of education or church position.

Those things can't cleanse anyone of their sins. We are the creature who can hurt our ministry work for the Lord if we are living in darkness in the church.

Church is all about the creator, God, who will not bend or break His law for any creature great or small.

The church is for all creatures to worship the true and only living God, who gave all creatures His only begotten Son.

He is living up in heaven and will come back again to take all of the righteous creatures back with him.

Beyond the fall of the first Adam, Jesus Christ our Lord is the second Adam and is without sin.

He is the living door for all God-like creatures to walk through to be saved before it's too late.

We Can Lay Down and Rest

The beautiful grass will lay down on the ground and rest so peacefully twenty-four hours around the clock.

The clouds will lay down across the sky and rest on a cloudy day that will stand by and watch.

You and me can lay down all of our burdens to rest in the Lord, who gives us a wake-up call of His will for us to do every day.

We belong to Jesus Christ, our Lord and savior. His almighty, strong hand can grip our souls tight and pull us out of our spiritual sleep.

It is never good for us to rest in this sour and cold world.

We can't afford to lay down our hearts and rest in the temporary things day after day.

You and I can lay down our trust and rest in Jesus Christ, who laid down his life on the cross and became sin to save us from our sins.

As Jesus laid down in the grave and rested from all of his works, he did not give up.

It is for us to lay down in God's grace and rest our souls so we find salvation in our risen savior who represents our case.

Great

A great speech can cheer a million people and make them believe that every word is true and they receive it with gladness.

An uneducated man can be misunderstood and overlooked by everyone.

The words of great people stand out in the limelight, but the words of small people can mean nothing.

What they say doesn't sound right to the ears of the rich and powerful, even though they themselves speak foolish words.

When a meek, poor person speaks words of wisdom, only a few people may hear.

It can mean nothing to a great person day after day.

Many great people believe the words of the small are cheap, rusty and broken, and that they're spoken from the gutter.

But, a great speech can be so vain, like counterfeit money.

If the holy and precious name of Jesus Christ is never spoken and lifted in a great speech by a great person who can influence millions of people then it's not a great speech to Jesus.

God's holy word is great and filled with truth to teach both the great and small.

So Extraordinary

When I was a little child, I was taught to say momma and daddy.

That sounded so good to me day after day.

As I grew older, the names momma and daddy had no blame because they sounded so right and were so right to me every day and every night.

I would say momma and daddy so brave, believing they could save me from anything going wrong in my life.

One day, for the first time, I heard the name Jesus Christ.

That name sounded so extraordinary and better than momma and daddy, even though they held me in their hands and it felt so good.

As I got older, I heard that name Jesus, sounding so meek and mild and so high above momma and daddy, who lifted me up so good.

They could never lift me up like Jesus Christ, who lifts me up to an extraordinary height that momma and daddy could never do.

A Reality Check from the Lord

A reality check from the Lord can be a painful experience.

Seeing one's own true self, who can never fool the Lord, who knows that you and I can fool ourselves into believing we're good and all right with Him.

The Lord will always see through our hearts so crystal clear every day. Jesus knows our every thought, motive and intent to be so sweet or sour to Him.

Whenever the Lord shows us our real, true selves we should thank Him and be glad that He hasn't left us all along.

We deceive ourselves thinking that we're in His favor, when we judge others' sins when we are not without sin and may hold grudges like we have every right to do so because we believe we're better than others.

A reality check from the Lord is there for us. The Lord never holds another person accountable for our sins.

No one can ever give you and me a complete reality check like the Lord can. He can set us free from lying to ourselves.

Most of us lie to ourselves more than we lie to anyone else.

We each have our own cross to carry as we follow Jesus Christ through the wilderness of our hearts.

If we don't have the Holy Spirit in us, our reality check will be a painful experience, but if we do have it then we can't deceive ourselves and will be encouraged to confess and repent of our sins.

The Lord gives us a reality check so we can stand up and face adversity and be bold and strong.

You and I have to accept the truth about ourselves.

If we do, Jesus will always care about saving our souls, without a doubt.

A reality check from the Lord is a shout of freedom to our souls.

Go and Tell People

Go and tell people about Jesus in a sermon, no matter whether it's in English, Spanish, French or German.

Go and tell people about Jesus in a song to build them up and make them strong.

Go and tell people so they will know spiritual things about Jesus Christ the king of kings.

Go and tell people about Jesus in a testimony that can touch people's hearts and make them know the sinless man, the Son of God whose kingdom will forever stand.

Go and tell people about Jesus Christ in your actions and show that you have been cleansed of your sins in Jesus' precious blood that was shed for us on the cross.

Go and tell people that Jesus paid for us to be saved, no matter how many times we are tossed up and down in our lives that should all be about Jesus Christ.

We Should Never Act Like…

We should never act like we are doing Jesus a favor by worshipping Him.

He is the savior of eternal life and is beyond you and me.

Our lives should be spent worshiping Him.

We should never act like we are entitled to heaven through our works. Jesus will turn his back on our works and call them vain if we try to manipulate the feeble-minded with selfish motives.

Doing that won't make us right with Jesus and we will not have his favor.

We should never act like we need to live to play the church or play God's Son as if we can set people free by our good works and what we say.

We are judged by what we say and do, and all good things come from Jesus Christ. He calls everyone to repent, great and small.

We should never act like we own ourselves or think we're more clever than the Lord.

He knows people's hearts.

When we don't fully know our own hearts, He will still know.

We should never act like we are so good and right all the time or judge others.

They might have favor with Jesus, regardless of whether we think they may not have a good name.

Jesus can bless us in his own time — that no one can change.

We should never act like we can predict who is lost and who is found in Jesus's name.

Depart From Me, I Never Knew You

One day someone asked me so bluntly, "Who are you?" I had to think before I responded to the question. I didn't want to answer in a bad tone of voice, to ease that person's mind.

It's never wrong to ask someone who they are. We don't want Jesus to tell us that He is finished and done with our excuses to not give Him our whole hearts. That can cause Jesus to say, "Depart from me. I never knew you. You trusted your own ways and not My ways."

If anyone wants to know who Jesus Christ is, the bible will tell you so much about Him and that He is the way, the truth and life eternal. His love will not depart from you and me. Knowing who Jesus is gives us a personal relationship with Him.

You and I will sometimes ask Jesus, "Who are you in our trials that can test us?"

You can score high in favor with man and can score in no favor with Jesus? If you hold onto unconfessed and unrepented sins, you will go your separate way from Jesus. Those who know Jesus would never do this.

Only Jesus can say, "Depart from me, I never knew you." He surely knows a pretender never knew Him, no matter how much good work is being done in His name. Jesus can deeply touch and change a heart once a person knows Him.

Believers will not depart from Him, even in the shadow of death. Death knew Jesus in the grave, but He told death, "Depart from Me, I never knew you," and He rose again to cleanse us of our sins.

No Excuse to Sin Against the Lord

If a man leaves his wife, she has no excuse to sin against the Lord. She can pray to Him in troubled times and the Lord will give her the strength to be faithful to Him, her spiritual husband. He will set her free from loneliness and insecurity.

If a woman leaves her husband, he has no excuse to sin against the Lord. He can pray to Him in his loneliness and insecurity. The Lord will give him the strength to do right by the bible every day and every night. The lord will not leave him or forsake him.

If a child is mature enough to know right from wrong, then that child can choose to trust the Lord and not sin against Him. If he or she is being bullied in school every day and feeling hurt and down about his parents being separated or divorced, he has no excuse to sin against the Lord.

No one has an excuse to sin against the Lord. The devil can't force anyone to speak evil words and do evil things unless they want to — that is our free will choice.

No one can say that he or she made me do this or that when we all can choose to not to give in to fear, that we can see so clear in the bible. Peter gave into fear and denied Jesus Christ three times, and Elijah gave into fear and hid himself from Jezebel who could not find him.

If someone doesn't love you and me in the church and loves to play tricks on us, we have no excuse to sin against the Lord, who will stick closer to us than a brother.

Satan Called God a Liar

In the Garden of Eden, Satan spoke through the serpent and called God a liar in front of Eve. She fell for Satan's lie, when she could've chosen to leave and move away from the tree of knowledge and good and evil and never go back to it on any day.

Eve was so amazed by what she saw and heard when the beautiful serpent was talking to her that she never heard from God and Adam.

"If you eat my fruit, you will surely not die," Satan said to Eve, who watched the serpent eat the delicious fruit, probably right down to the core.

Satan told eve that she would be like God and know what is good and evil and have supernatural powers that were equal with God's.

Today, Satan is still calling God a liar in front of us, telling us not to trust God and his holy word that says Jesus Christ is the door to let us into heaven where Lucifer cannot enter because there is no grace for him.

God judged fairly and gave Lucifer a chance to repent. He was too late.

You and I do not want to be like Lucifer and wait until it's too late for us. That would be the biggest mistake anyone could ever make.

Satan is a liar every day. We can call Satan a liar before this world if we love and obey Jesus Christ, the Son of God, beyond the gates of everlasting pearls.

In the Universe of Our Hearts

There are endless stars of thoughts in the universe of our hearts that brings on galaxies of motives needing the gravity of God's goodness.

God leads our hearts to repentance on His holy ground. God can go to the ends of the universe in our hearts and walk around the solar systems of our choices traveling through the light years of our conscious. God sees the shooting stars near the centers of our destiny.

He is the space shuttle traveling through the outer space of our free will. God made it known to other worlds that He is love and is fair.

He leaves us to choose Him to keep us on the right course in the universe of our hearts. God doesn't force anyone to love Him, who keeps the outer space from being lost in the space of His eternal heart that is the source of our soul's salvation.

Woman

Beautiful, pretty, fine, gorgeous, attractive and cute is from her head to her feet in the eyes of her beholder from sun up to sun down.

Her presence is magnetic in so many eyes every day and her intelligence is very high, like a mountain.

Woman is her sweet and wonderful name, and her love is an eternal flame that never burns out in this world.

A man can't blame a woman for his own mistakes.

This world has so much pain that her strength can soothe. A man is not whole without her love that is a great wealth to behold and can't be sold.

If a man could live without a woman, God wouldn't have created a woman for us men.

We got the greatest gift from God over all the other creatures on earth.

New galaxies give birth to infinite stars in the universe. A woman can carry life in her precious womb and birth a baby in the image of God, who created all things for His glory.

Life would have nothing good to give and life would have no good true story to tell if there were no women living on this earth.

We men would become desolate without them, and wander in the wilderness alone. All men would eventually end up dead and become fossils without women.

Jesus's best friend on earth was a woman in his life.

From One Place to the Next Place

A bird can fly from one place to the next place.

Feelings can stay in one place and not touch base with reality.

We can go from one place to the next place when our minds can stay in one place and take a true fact out of context.

We can make a choice to stay in one place day by day, but our dreams can move from one place to the next place in our deep sleep.

We can sit in one place in a car that can take us from one place to the next place, near and far.

Our brains will stay in one place in our skulls, but our thoughts can go from one place to the next place without a dull thought.

You and I can go from one place to the next place, but our body parts will stay in one place no matter how many flaws we have.

Change can move from one place to the next place in different generations.

God's law will stay in one place to point out our sins.

We can take the bible from one place to the next place, and our soul's salvation will stay in one place for us to make our calling sure in Jesus Christ, who knows that if we are saved in Him we won't be lost in our sins below heaven from one place to the next place.

Light

A car light can flash by us and disappear down a dark street.

A flashlight can have a dim light because the batteries are weak.

A shadow can appear where there is some light, but will disappear when the light goes out.

The sunlight will shine so bright all day long.

A light bulb can blow out in the house

The full white moonlight can glow all night long.

The light on a lightning bug glows in our eyes and in our hands.

Throughout the outer space of infinite light years the stars will shine their little sparkles of light from afar.

If we could get close to those stars, they would be so much bigger than some planets that we can't go to.

Jesus Christ, our Lord, has given you and me a light to shine his gospel truth in a dark world so that everyone will see the light of the world shining in us.

If we love Jesus and keep his laws, then that belief will shine through a dark heart and cause him to want to meet Jesus.

Wise Up

You can only wise up for yourself. You can chose to fear God and keep His commandments every day, week, month and year.

No one else can wise up for you or me.

In this world where it's so easy to say and do something foolish and not see it's bad side effects. We have to be in the right frame of mind to choose to wise up and love everyone the same, especially in the household of faith.

Every child of God is not always so wise about giving Jesus Christ a true heart of repentance and obedience.

In this sinful world, everyone who is at a mature age is not wise about denying self and coming boldly to an all-wise God whose foolishness is wiser than men will ever know.

We will never know the Lord God to ever say or do something foolish against His own ten golden rules of eternal wisdom: love, peace, joy and truth. He will bless our lives with health and strength every day.

You and I can study a holy book filled with God's wisdom, and we can pray and ask the Lord for wisdom in this vile world where many adults are more foolish than a child.

Countless Raindrops

We cannot count the raindrops falling from the sky high above the ground.

Raindrops fall down into our eyes and we cannot see all of the raindrops falling so free from the sky that hovers over you and me.

Day after day God's blessings are countless, like the raindrops falling from the clouds in the sky high above the highest mountaintop.

God's raindrops of mercy are so countless, falling upon our lives every day under the sign of the rainbow arching over you and me.

We cannot count how many times God blesses us under the sunshine where raindrops are countless.

We don't care about counting the raindrops, we are just glad the rain is cooling off a hot day.

No one doubts that it's right for the rain to fall from the sky and be so merciful upon the hot, dry land.

Raindrops will fall on countlessly, just like Jesus has won our battles for us.

We can surely thank God for giving us His Son to save us from our countless sins. He makes them gone like no more rain falling from the sky for the sun to come out with countless rays of light, shining on you and me.

We know there is no wrong that God can do.

Jesus Gave

Jesus gave equality to the Samarian woman who he met at the water well.

Jesus didn't think that he was too good to ask her for some water to drink.

Jesus gave justice to the woman who was caught in adultery. She was brought to him to see if He would stone her to death.

Jesus Christ didn't do this. He forgave her of her sins and encouraged her to live a renewed life.

Jesus gave freedom to large crowds of people who He healed from the slavery of sickness, diseases and demon possession that is real today.

Jesus gave everyone the opportunity to come to Him and get set free from living in sins that can enslave you and me and make the devil our master.

Jesus gave peace to his disciples when they saw him after He rose from the grave and went to where they were. They saw him with nail prints in His hands.

Jesus gave God's love to even the Pharisees and soldiers who crucified Him on the cross, where He hung and said, "Father forgive them for they know not what they do."

What was wrong, God made right to show all the world His love for all men.

There is No Abandonment in the Lord

Many people have abandoned their spouses and children, even when they're living in the same house.

Family members can be abandoned emotionally and spiritually under the same roof.

Selfishness can abandon trust and unity to bring on strife and disharmony in a house. That means it's not a home.

If the husband or wife or both have abandoned the Lord, this means they've abandoned their own souls' salvation. This is the worst kind of abandonment. They are going cold turkey on the Lord and being selfish by going their own way and living to please only themselves.

They will reap what they sow.

This can happen whether they are poor, middle class or rich.

This behavior can open the door and invite the abandonment of sin.

There is no abandonment in the Lord Jesus Christ, who will always care and supply all of our needs. We will never get weary of well-doing unto Him. He also shows His mercy to fools who abandon him.

He can't fail to comfort us and strengthen us in our abandonment of trials. That is fair to us in Jesus' name.

If Jesus Had

If Jesus had stayed in heaven above, this world wouldn't know anything about God's love, given to all the world through his Son, Jesus Christ.

If Jesus had committed one sin in his life, then God would be a liar. God cannot lie, and his Son saved us, thus we should believe in God.

If Jesus had come into this world wearing a white robe and crown, no one would know what it means to humble oneself and bow down.

If God had made it possible for Jesus to not drink the cup of his wrath against sin, then God wouldn't be love and we couldn't be redeemed back to him when this world ends.

If Jesus had not put on the flesh of men, we wouldn't have desire to stop living in our sins. Jesus can give our flesh the power to overcome.

If Jesus had not humbled himself unto death, God would not blot out our sins and no one would be worth saving. This would mean that God's grace would be a waste of time under the sun.

If Jesus had stayed in the grave, there would be no you and me and no church today. We wouldn't know to love and obey Jesus and always pray to Jesus. He wouldn't hear us and answer our prayers.

If Jesus was dead, the bible would be worthless and no one would believe.

If Jesus had not crushed the serpent's head, upon our death we would all be permanently dead.

Who, What, When, Where, How and Why

Who am I? Who will know me? God's holy word can surely tell me more than one half and three thirds of me. It is there for me to know the whole me.

What is God's purpose for me? I can't choose my own purpose. I will be judged by the Son of God, all alone, to be saved or lost.

When will I deny all of me? I have a choice to do right or wrong this very day. I will set my destiny course on the road of my heart.

Where can I always find the best and worst of me? Only the Lord can always find me and lead me far beyond the worst of me, to be the best in Him.

How can the best filmmaker in this world film my thoughts? Only God know my thoughts and will film all of my motives and intents in my heart. He will decide whether to call me a Christian or a hypocrite.

Why must I examine myself and work out my own soul's salvation? No one else can carry my cross for me. I have no excuse to not know.

Why can't God lie to me? Because he is the truth, but my sinful nature will always lie to me and tell me I cannot to be saved in Jesus Christ, who is alive for me.

The Beauty of Wisdom

Wisdom is so very beautiful, like a princess and queen. This is the beauty of wisdom, looking so fine and lean as she walks down the streets of life.

Ignorance will stare at her beauty with nothing to say.

Wisdom will care to help ignorance wise up and make the right choices.

Foolishness will envy her beauty in the day and night.

Wisdom will shine like the sun and full white moonlight, as she walks down the streets of life.

Knowledge sees her beautiful face, as if it were a hidden treasure found. One that opens up and is filled with gold, diamonds, rubies and pearls of good advice.

Knowledge knows that even an educated fool will make bad choices.

So beautiful, like a stunning woman, is wisdom with her beautiful, bright eyes.

Looking through the ways of fools, who speak out against God's holy word and break God's ten golden rules.

Wisdom will not flaunt her beauty like a woman attracting attention to herself.

Should Not be Surprised

If I trust Jesus, I should not be surprised about what the Lord can do for you in my eyes.

If you trust Jesus, you should not be surprised about what the Lord can do for me.

There are many people who are surprised about the Lord's blessings and who He wants to bless.

We can doubt one another when we get a miraculous blessing from the Lord, but if we're born again believers in Jesus Christ we should not be surprised about how the Lord can bless someone's life.

If we are surprised about what the Lord Jesus can do for you and me or anyone else, then we surely have a lack of trust in Jesus. He can do the impossible for us.

If we truly believe that Jesus cannot fail, we should not be surprised that He can change the bad in us and bless us to be good.

All the Hardships

All the hardships that you brought me through, O Lord, seem like a dream that you woke me out of to give You more and more of the glory and praise that You alone deserve.

All of my past, present and future days, you own, beyond all of my mistakes that you, my Lord Jesus Christ, did not allow to bury me down it the ground where there is no life to live.

I am so glad to still be alive to make the devil mad about you, O Lord, being there for me so he can't go against me.

I truly know for myself when I should have been dead in the eyes of my enemies a long time ago, but you were right there by my side and winked your eye at my ignorance. You let me live in the knowledge of Your truth. You set me free from myself.

I must pick up my cross and follow You today like there was no yesterday and no tomorrow to come my way.

Pride will not keep me from being Godly. I know the hardships You brought me through, O Lord, and I will glorify You.

Will Not Change

The Lord will not change His word for anyone's feelings that can come and go on any day.

That temptation can look so appealing, especially to anyone who doesn't have a relationship with the Lord. He will not change His word for anyone's desires.

We can end up with a bad deal if we don't yield to God's holy word, even though it won't change for anyone great or small.

The Lord's word is for all to live by in a sinful world of so many people making up their own definitions of what love is.

They are so far away from God's golden rules of love and don't keep his holy word that runs deep in a repentant heart.

Those who believe leap for joy unto the Lord Jesus Christ, who overcame the world's ways of selfish living that the bible is against each and every day.

Our Lord and savior Jesus Christ will not change his holy word for anyone. Follow it and you will not miss out on the bliss of heaven.

Those who are living against God's bible word will find that the Lord will take no risks and won't change one dot or tilt on his word. We are meant to forever obey God.

Will Flow

The rivers will flow into the oceans so smooth.

Our ways can flow into selfishness so unseen and cool.

The strong winds will cause the ocean waves to roar.

Strong anger can cause emotions to roar beyond the closed doors.

The rivers will flow into the oceans so very sure every day.

Our thoughts can flow into words so very sure to say something good or something bad.

The full white moon will glow its night light so mysterious upon the deep waters.

Time will flow so uncertain in our lives.

The rivers will flow into the oceans so nice.

So many people are living their lives so wild, like a beast not tamed.

The ocean waters will stretch for miles and miles and stay in place like a good little child.

The heart can stretch for good or evil, for miles and miles, and stay in its place to bless the land or curse it.

The rivers will flow into the oceans in unity for all to see.

Everyone who loves and obeys Jesus Christ will not fall into a destiny that can flow into Hell. We know our divine call to God.

Visitor

The trees will get many visitors like insects, so will the bushes, trees and grass.

Insects love to hang out in these areas as long as they can last.

The church should always be a place for visitors to always come to and get set free from their burdens by giving them to the Lord.

You and I can get bitten by the insects of sin that love to visit our minds and draw our thoughts away from Jesus, where they need to be all the time.

There are a lot of bad visitors in this world, where not everyone is there to help us. Many are there to mess up your life and mock you.

Jesus loves to visit our hearts around the clock.

Jesus will visit us every day with his holy ghost if we love him the most and gladly boast about him who is worthy to be praised.

No visitor on earth is more glorious than Jesus, who will come to stay in our lives when a visitor can come and go away.

Jesus is the Truth

Jesus is the truth that many people don't believe. Instead, they truly believe a lie and get deceived.

If anyone takes a lie detector test and says that he has no sins and passes the test, then the lie detector is a lie.

Only Jesus Christ lived on earth without sin in his flesh. The bible says this is true and the bible will always pass the lie detector test.

In this world, a lie can fool many people, but it can never fool Jesus, who saw through all the devil's lies to set you and me free with His truth.

A lie can appear to be the truth like a wolf in sheep's clothing.

Jesus is the shepherd of his true sheep for keeps.

Jesus is the truth that cannot lie in His holy word.

Will Disappear

A child can disappear and go missing for years and years.

None of Jesus' children will ever go missing from His heart, where he holds every missing child, teenager and adult so dear.

The morning will disappear into the afternoon.

The afternoon will disappear into the evening.

The evening will disappear into the night.

This world will one day disappear too, into a new world where no sorrow and tears will ever exist because the Lord will make sin disappear.

A shadow will disappear in the bright sunlight that shines so clear.

Jesus will never disappear His law from this world.

The summer will disappear into the fall, and the fall will disappear into winter, which will disappear into spring.

Jesus will never disappear His real salvation to all who are saved in Him.

Time

Time is not always on our side. Time loves for us to be faithful and true to Jesus Christ our Lord, who can be merciful when time may not be kind to us.

We must let time run its course because we can't outrun time. This we know with no doubt.

If we wait on the Lord, time is always good at running its course.

We are not always good at trusting time from the Lord, who created time to run its course in our lives.

Nothing in this world can overcome obstacles like time that it takes to learn from our mistakes. This is not too hard to do on any day.

The Lord will forgive us through His saving grace.

Time can be a good friend to us if we don't waste it chasing behind temporary things.

Jesus is eternal, and time knows that Jesus is its king.

Caught Up

Like a bug being caught up in a spider's web, we can get caught up in the things of the world that will make us spiritually ill.

Being caught up in the Lord will knock down any spiritual spider web laying a trap for us and we will not get caught up in it.

Like a bear's claws getting caught up in a bear trap, we can get caught up in getting revenge that can snap our claw of trust in Jesus.

Trusting Jesus can change someone's life and make them a good person who will do right by Him.

Like a gang being caught up in recruiting new members, you and I can get caught up in following through on something that is not the right thing to do.

Jesus will always know when we are blind spiritually and can't see what's wrong.

Getting caught up in Jesus, who can set us free from our selfish ways, is where we should be caught up.

Kindness

There are a lot of kind people in this world we live in, especially little boys and girls.

Children need a kind friend in school to help them through their day.

Kindness can mend broken hearts and heal.

Kindness can get rid of grudges and lend a helping hand.

Kindness will usually get people's attention and cause them to be nice in return, regardless of how we look.

Being kind can entice a mean person to want to try being nice for a change.

All who love the Lord know that it's not a strange thing to be kind, even to our enemies who may surely believe that it's strange to be kind to them.

Don't be deceived, kindness is of the Lord, who is always so kind to you and me every day under the sunshine.

If the Lord wasn't kind to us, we would never have peace of mind.

There is Never Enough

There is never enough of praying and worshipping the Lord.

There is never enough of witnessing for the Lord here and there and everywhere we go from day to day.

There is never enough of working for the Lord.

We will never get enough of His love, mercy and grace day after day.

There is never enough of loving the Lord Jesus Christ, who is forever more clever than the devil, who will never get enough of tempting us to sin against the Lord.

The Lord will never get enough of being our best friend until the end of our lives.

We should never get enough of living by God's holy word.

Jesus will never get enough of giving to us to live right.

There is never enough of confessing and repenting of our sins unto the Lord, who we can always trust.

We will never get enough of our Lord Jesus Christ before we lick the dust of the grave that will never get enough of the dead.

Life will never get enough of our living unto Jesus Christ.

Can Talk

What we wear can talk good or bad to people before we say one word from the tip of our tongues day after day.

Our eyes can talk good or bad to people who can look in our eyes and may see kindness, pride, judgment or sour hatred.

How we act can talk good or bad to people who have sense enough to know if they are liked or disliked.

What we eat can talk good or bad to people who may not know what is good or not good to eat.

What we drink can talk good or bad to people in the home and on the streets where everyone might not know what is good or bad to drink.

The company that we keep can talk good or bad to people and make them think good or bad about us.

Before we say one word about Jesus Christ, people will see the way that we live our lives and whether we're good or bad.

Living for Jesus, our Lord, is always a good example for people to think about walking through the church doors.

Does the Lord Ever Get Tired?

Birds can get tired of flying and land on the ground, in a tree or in the water to rest from their long flight.

You and I can get tired and need a good night's sleep under the sky.

Children can get tired of playing, and their eyes can look sleepy. This lets their parents know they need to take a nap.

Animals can get tired of searching for food that they can't wait to eat when they're hungry. They'll leave no food behind.

The Lord can get tired of suffering long for you and me, waiting for us to repent of our sins and let Him live in our hearts.

The Lord can get tired of us sinning against Him, but He will never get tired of giving sinners His love.

He can get tired of you and me making excuses for our sins day after day.

The Lord does get tired of people rejecting His holy spirit and moving away from Him and leaning to their own ways of living instead of living according to His word.

In All of Us

There is a mystery in all of us.

Our hearts are not too deep for God to understand and make known.

God's goodness can reach way down into the depths of our hearts and wake us from our spiritual sleep.

There is a destiny for all of us who will created our destiny by the deeds we do — good or bad.

The Lord God, who's image is in all of us, has taught us to reason like Him.

There is the breath of God in all of us who are alive and turn away from self to live unto Jesus Christ our Lord, who's worthy of our praise.

There is a need in all of us to be in accord with God, like the angels in heaven above all of us.

We all have sins that God sees, but he gave His Son to set all of us free from our sins.

All of us should confess and repent and let Jesus live in us and make us right with God

God can put his time in all of us and give us a chance to be saved before it's too late.

Sin is in all of us to go to the grave.

No One but You and Your Partner

Someone left a play script on your desk with a note saying:

> This is your script to rehearse. You will be a part of a play at the theatre next week. You have a choice to be real or just play-act your script with an unknown partner on the stage under the limelight.

You are excited about playing your part and you memorize the words in the script that you must say to your unknown partner. Without a second thought, you are determined to be on that stage floor at the theatre to perform your act.

The week you had to rehearse your script is over. You show up at the back entrance of the theatre and knock on the door.

Someone lets you in, and you dress up in your costume in the dressing room.

You come out of your dressing room to stand behind the tall curtains. Then someone approaches you and asks if you are ready to perform your part.

You say, "Yes, I am," while being so excited to meet your partner for the first time.

The curtains open under the bright limelight and you walk confidently onto the stage floor.

Suddenly you are so shocked to see there is no audience in the theatre — it's empty — and you're so disappointed.

Then, you see Jesus walking toward you on the stage floor to meet with you alone in the theatre.

This is your moment to be real with Jesus or just play-act your script.

Jesus Christ is always real with you and me.

Jesus is our lifetime partner.

We should know not to be shocked when we see Him on the clouds of glory some day soon.

The New Jerusalem Holy City

I dreamed about a beautiful city that stretched for miles and miles.

It had a glamorous view, which I observed with a big smile on my face.

As I journeyed through that beautiful city, I didn't want to leave because I was so happy to be there.

My eyes were full of amazement, seeing great perfect places of peace, joy and love that never ceased from the east to the west.

That beautiful city I saw in my dream was empty, but would one day be filled up with people with no sins to pollute it.

This was the city that Jesus Christ created and He will live there with all of his righteous children. They will have residence there for doing God's holy will.

In this old sinful world, where sin is in every city, country, state and town, people can believe in Jesus Christ and be saved so they can one day live in the New Jerusalem holy city. It is very real, beyond dreams that Jesus can use to show us so clear.

This world is so near to the end, and that holy city will soon be fulfilled.

We Can

We can lay so still in our sleep and run from place to place in our dreams, like an escaped fugitive on the run.

It can be quiet in our house and noisy in our thoughts.

We can't always get away from getting caught by guilt in our hearts, we can speak good words of love and part away from the Lord in our motives and intents.

We can fail to truly confess and repent of our sins unto the Lord, who is good all the time.

We can want to climb up the ladder to success and might not always see to love one another in the church where we can do good works and not be of the church.

We can look back at the things of the world like Lot's wife.

We can be greatly favored by human beings and still have no favor with God, who cannot lie.

We can lie to ourselves if we believe that we can save ourselves and make the cross look so vain.

The grave knows that the righteous dead are saved in Jesus Christ, who will always do so much more for us than we can ever do for ourselves under the great blue sky.

On the Run

There was a rich man who had everything he ever wanted to have.

He had many houses, cars, trucks, boats and airplanes.

He had tons of shoes and clothes and even an empire of businesses.

He had so much money that he could fill up a thousand bank vaults.

Then one day he got very sick and was in so much physical pain that he was paralyzed and confined to his bed.

He cried out to his houses and cars to take away his pain and save him. He got no answer.

Then he screamed out loud to his airplanes, clothes and shoes to ease his pain. He still received no answer.

He lay in his bed so hopeless and made one last cry to his empire of businesses and all of his money, asking that they rescue him from his pain and grief. Yet, still, he got no answer.

Everyone in his life was trying to get away from him and his selfish ways, so there was no person to answer him either.

The rich man finally wised up and cried out to God to take away his unbearable pain. God answered him and said, "You have been on the run from me and in the process caused everyone in your life to run away from you. You must give yourself over to Me, and I will ease your pain."

Nothing To and Something To

What may seem to be nothing to you and me may be a lot to someone else who might not have a pot to cook food in and might not have food to eat.

You and I always need to be thankful unto the Lord for everything that belongs to Him day after day, no matter where you live or what you experience in your life.

That means something to us, especially when we are sick and feel so crushed, but may seem to be nothing to someone who is well. They'll take it for granted.

We can't take Jesus for granted. If we're not being thankful to Jesus Christ and acknowledging him as the king of kings and Lord of Lords in our life, we aren't living right.

If we are making Jesus Christ our choice day after day, that will mean nothing to the wicked, whose lives are full of ungratefulness unto the Lord.

We are all something through His grace, and the devil is nothing under the stars.

Addicted

Being addicted to loving Jesus Christ is a good addiction in anyone's life.

Jesus saves us from being addicted to living in sin.

Many people are addicted to fame and want to make a great name for themselves in this world.

Some are addicted to persecuting people in Jesus' name.

Many people are addicted to material things that are temporary below heaven above where Jesus is king of kings.

The holy angels are addicted to Jesus forever and ever.

Being addicted to Jesus is a good addiction that can never be bad for our mental and physical health.

Being addicted to bad substances can shorten our lives and lead to an early death.

Jesus has victory over death. He rose from the grave with his breath of eternal life. He was addicted to doing his heavenly Father's will.

You and I can get addicted to doing our own will, which is a real spiritual addiction that can cause our souls to be lost.

Jesus is addicted to saving our souls so we can live in heaven with Him one day and fill God's heart with joy.

There is No Way to Get Around

There is no way to get around God's holy word, no matter who we are or where we live day after day throughout our lives.

We can't pass by God's word and do our own will and lean to our own ways. Doing that will get us into some real trouble. Sooner rather than later we will regret it because there is no way to get around God's holy word. It is here, there and everywhere we go.

God's word is like a double-edged sword. It cuts up our motives, thoughts, words and actions for being so wrong and sour.

The Lord, our God and savior, Jesus Christ gives us power to resist temptation that can seem so right and can cause us to feel so good. This will shorten our lives to lick the dust. If we live our lives disobeying God's holy word, that we can trust to direct us every day to confess our sins and repent.

We can't get around and above God, because Jesus is our door to heaven.

God's holy word is about Jesus Christ, who will never let us get around one tilt or dot of His word that is life every day to our renewed life through God's grace.

God is being so nice to give us a chance to be saved in Jesus Christ.

Promise

If I make you a promise, I must keep it. If you make me a promise, you must keep it, too.

My word is my bond and your word is your bond. Make no mistake, this is the way it is under the sun, every day and every night.

There are good promises and bad promises, and we can fail to follow through on either of them even though we mean well.

God, on the other hand, cannot fail us and will follow through on his promise.

We can still stand on our feet even if we fall, as long as we repent of our sins unto Jesus Christ who is God's living eternal promise to you and me.

If we live our lives as a promise to God by loving Jesus and obeying His holy laws, we will be saved.

If we do not do this, God promises us eternal death at the end of our lives.

Only Jesus can give you and me His promise of eternal life.

We Christians

We Christians are the most hated people in this world, even though we Christians are the most selfless people for all the world to see.

Everyday criminals are the most selfish people we will ever see in this world. Many criminals today are praised for their evil practices against what the bible says about our Lord and savior Jesus Christ who was the most selfless and hated man on earth.

Jesus was born of the Holy Ghost to be without sin in this flesh.

You and I should always boast about Him if we love Jesus in our voice and body.

Jesus humbled himself unto death and rose again for our names to be written in the book of life.

If we live a Christian life that is selfless, that the devil hates every day and every night, we will be saved.

God loves us Christians and will give us Christians the crown of eternal life through his Son, Jesus Christ.

Jesus found us and asks us to come to Him in this sinful world where all who are lost can't blame a Christian and surely not the Lord, who has no flaws.

Broken

Many dreams are broken, and that may be for a good reason.

Only Jesus always knows in every season.

Many people are so broken in their hearts.

Jesus didn't give us our hearts to rebel against Him.

He can mend broken hearts when they do his will.

What's good about something being broken?

A broken down car will let us know that it needs to be fixed.

All around this world, broken people are something good to the Lord.

He loves to fix broken people if they love and obey him. He's good all the time to all of us.

A glass can fall on the floor and break into pieces.

You and I can make our lives to be broken if we don't love Jesus Christ, who can glue our lives back together with His super glue of life eternal.

Jesus was broken on the cross to fix you and me when the devil loves breaking us up into pieces of sinning against God.

Jesus paid the price for us broken people with is life.

A Trial Date with God

Everybody in this world has a trial date with God.

Your trial date or my trial date might be today.

God will open someone's case in his divine courtroom up in heaven and Jesus Christ will be our lawyer. He will represent you and me and God will give us a fair trial, judging us for all of our deeds here on earth.

Everybody has a trial date to meet God one-on-one along with Jesus, the Son of God, who will give you and me a chance to know that God's judgment is fair and real to all great and small, saved and not saved.

Everybody who ever lived will be judged by God, to decide whether you will be a citizen of heaven or a citizen of hell.

One day, when we least expect it, our trial date will come.

Only Jesus knows the heat of God's wrath upon all who are lost in this world.

Everybody has a verdict beyond all the courtrooms and judges on earth.

If We Don't Say

If we don't say a word, our body language will say something so real.

Jesus Christ, our Lord, will always have something to say to us in his holy word, day after day.

The bible's language is very real.

If we don't say anything, then no one knows what is on our minds. The mind of Jesus is in His holy word.

Jesus will always say something right at the right time.

If we don't say one word, our lives will say something about us making the right or wrong choices.

We can always trust to live our lives in Jesus.

If we don't say anything at all, our silence can be heard in our actions, obeying the law or not obeying the law.

Our actions will always say something before someone else who may or may not love and obey the Lord.

If we say nothing to Jesus, he knows our hearts that talk with loud motives that He will always see, regardless of whether we walk the walk or talk the talk.

Jesus

A memory and a thought can fade away.

If we think on Jesus, he will be worthy of our day.

No matter if we don't remember every word that we say.

A beautiful, sunny day and a smile can light up someone's life for them to go the extra mile.

Jesus can light up our lives, if we dial him up and talk to him from our hearts.

A bubble can burst and be nowhere to be found ever again.

Our lives are like that bubble to Jesus, who has no end. We can burst like a bubble if we don't believe in Jesus Christ who finds us.

No animal would harm itself or take its own life.

Jesus created us in His own image. Why should we take our own life?

You and I should love doing His will.

A ball can bounce and roll.

Life can bounce us and roll us like a ball, but Jesus can pick us up and hold us in his hands that all the saints will never be thrown back and forth in.

Our Works

If we had to work our way to heaven, it would never be good enough for God.

You and I are so unworthy before God, who sees our righteousness as filthy rags that we may see as a full bag of beautiful red apples ready to be placed in a bowl on the table for people's eyes to embrace.

We can compare ourselves with one another and compare our works to see if we're more highly qualified and acceptable before the Lord than someone else. We can look down on people and think they're of no use to God.

It's always good to hold others in higher esteem than ourselves. The Lord shows no respect to good works in His name when we're sinners.

Our works can't cleanse us of our sins — no matter what good we do, it can't cleanse us.

Pride can fill us and make us believe that Jesus needs us, as if the price he paid for us was in vain.

There is no love in boasting about ourselves. We can't make ourselves right with God and we can't rise above God, no matter how great we think our works are.

Our good works can be good enough to be like silver and gold in one another's eyes, but God sees our works and views them like a rusty can filled with filthy water.

The good works of Jesus are always right with God.

In the Sand of My Life

O Lord, You carry me through my tears with Your footprints in the sand of my life being so dear to You day after day.

O Lord, You carry me through my grief with your footprints in the sand of my life. My belief in your is real to me.

O Lord, You carry me through my joy with your footprints in the sand of my life that You will lift me up with a smile on my face to help someone else to smile.

O Lord, You carry me through every mile in my heart with your footprints in the sand of my life that I need to always love You, my Lord and savior Jesus Christ.

O Lord, You carry me through the land of the living with your footprints in the sand of my life that will always be meant to do Your will that I was born to do to have good sense.

O Lord, You carry me through my choices with Your footprints in the sand of my life that I can choose or not choose to sin against You, my Lord Jesus Christ.

Is Like the Wide-Open Sky

Our mind is like the wide-open sky to God who sees every thought flying by like a bird in the sky.

Our heart is like the wide-open sky to God who sees every motive flying near and far like a bird in the sky.

Our life is like the wide-open sky to God who knows where our life will fly to from day to day below the heavens on high above the sky.

Our destiny is like the wide-open sky to God who sees every choice that we make to fly so free in the sunlight of God or in the darkness of the devil.

Our Purpose

What good purpose do we have in life, if we don't believe in Jesus Christ?

Whatever we say has no true purpose, if Jesus is not spoken on our tongues.

Whatever we do has no real purpose, if it's not for Jesus' name sake.

Our true purpose in life is to love and obey Jesus Christ each and every day.

Jesus made His purpose to save our souls from being lost in sin.

We can't change our real, true purpose, we shouldn't live our life to do our own thing.

If we don't live out our purpose for being here, we are better off never being born to grieve the holy spirit of God.

Our purpose is not our own to claim.

Life Can Make Us

Many will say that life is what you make it.

Life can make us change for the better or for the worse.

Life is living but life won't promise us to always have a good life.

Jesus Christ had once lived His life on earth. His life wasn't always good, even though His life was without sin.

We were born in sin for life to make us so vulnerable to heartaches, disappointments and grief.

Life can make us to question our life.

King Solomon was the wisest man to ever live, but he didn't fully understand life.

Only Jesus has the authority over life to command life to give us another day to live.

If we had control over life, no one would die at a young age.

Many good people die at a young age, and they didn't make their life that way.

Jesus Wants Our All

Jesus wants our all and He wants us to give it to Him.

My all is different from your all to give to Jesus.

My all may be two or three good things that I can give to Jesus.

Your all may be ten or twenty good things that you can give to Jesus.

Jesus looks at your all and my all as being the same, even though your all is more than my all.

Jesus doesn't want anything less than our all. That pleases Him.

Jesus will never compare your all with my all.

Jesus is not like a man, who can compare more or less talented or gifted.

If we don't give Jesus our all, no matter how much it is, then anything less means nothing to Him.

We can't Chase Behind Time

We can't chase behind time that can chase behind us and catch up with us.

We would run out of breath before we could catch up with time.

Time will always be ahead of us who don't know where time will lead us.

Only Jesus can chase behind our time here on earth.

He can always catch our time and stop it from shortening our lives.

Jesus will sometimes permit time to shorten many peoples' lives, especially if they are doing a lot of evil things.

We can't always question Jesus about why he let our loved ones die before their time.

Time won't question Jesus, who time can't chase behind and catch.

Time will always trust Jesus to give us time to chase behind and catch our salvation in Jesus Christ.

Time knows that only Jesus can save our souls.

We can't chase behind time and catch it.

Only Jesus can control time and make it stand still and wait on us to run towards Him and cross over the finish line of being saved before it's too late.

Who Can Be More?

Who can be more loving than God?

Who can be more holy than God?

Who can be more right than God?

Who can be more powerful than God?

Who can be more smart than God?

Who can be more joyful than God?

Who can be greater than God?

Who can be more beautiful than God?

Who can be bigger than God?

Who can be more peaceful than God?

Who can be more giving than God?

Who can be more free than God?

Who can be more truthful than God?

Who can be more successful than God?

Who can be higher than God?

Who can be more mysterious than God?

Who can be wiser than God?

Lucifer tried to be better than God. He failed to regret it forever and ever.

So, who are we to try to be more spiritual than God?

www.ingramcontent.com/pod-product-compliance
Lightning Source LLC
Chambersburg PA
CBHW071554080526
44588CB00010B/914